OPPOSING
VIEWPOINTS®
SERIES

W9-AHE-959

AIDS

Other Books of Related Interest:

Opposing Viewpoints Series

Epidemics
Health
Sexually Transmitted Diseases

Current Controversies Series

AIDS in Developing Countries
Do Abstinence Programs Work?
Teen Sex

At Issue Series

Disease Eradication
Medical Ethics

> "Congress shall make no law ... abridging the freedom of speech, or of the press."

First Amendment to the US Constitution

The basic foundation of our democracy is the First Amendment guarantee of freedom of expression. The Opposing Viewpoints Series is dedicated to the concept of this basic freedom and the idea that it is more important to practice it than to enshrine it.

OPPOSING
VIEWPOINTS®
SERIES

| AIDS

Roman Espejo, Book Editor

GREENHAVEN PRESS
A part of Gale, Cengage Learning

GALE
CENGAGE Learning·

Detroit • New York • San Francisco • New Haven, Conn • Waterville, Maine • London

Elizabeth Des Chenes, *Managing Editor*

© 2012 Greenhaven Press, a part of Gale, Cengage Learning

Gale and Greenhaven Press are registered trademarks used herein under license.

For more information, contact:
Greenhaven Press
27500 Drake Rd.
Farmington Hills, MI 48331-3535
Or you can visit our Internet site at gale.cengage.com.

For product information and technology assistance, contact us at:

Gale Customer Support, 1-800-877-4253.
For permission to use material from this text or product, submit all requests online at www.cengage.com/permissions.

Further permissions questions can be emailed to permissionrequest@cengage.com.

Articles in Greenhaven Press anthologies are often edited for length to meet page requirements. In addition, original titles of these works are changed to clearly present the main thesis and to explicitly indicate the author's opinion. Every effort is made to ensure the Greenhaven Press accurately reflects the original intent of the authors. Every effort has been made to trace the owners of copyrighted material.

Cover Image Derek P. Redfearn/The Image Bank/Getty Images.

LIBRARY OF CONGRESS CATALOGING-IN-PUBLICATION DATA

AIDS / book editor, Roman Espejo.
    p. cm. -- (Opposing viewpoints)
    Summary: "What Causes AIDS?; What Is the Status of the Global AIDS Epidemic?; How Can the Spread of AIDS Be Controlled?; How Should AIDS Be Treated?"-- Provided by publisher.
    Includes bibliographical references and index.
    ISBN 978-0-7377-5705-7 (hardback) -- ISBN 978-0-7377-5706-4 (paperback)
    1. AIDS (Disease)--Juvenile literature. I. Espejo, Roman, 1977-
    RC606.65.A33 2012
    616.97'92--dc23

                                         2011032930

Printed in the United States of America
1 2 3 4 5 6 7 16 15 14 13 12

APR 27 2012

Contents

Why Consider Opposing Viewpoints?

> "The only way in which a human being
> can make some approach to knowing
> the whole of a subject is by hearing
> what can be said about it by persons of
> every variety of opinion and studying
> all modes in which it can be looked at
> by every character of mind. No wise
> man ever acquired his wisdom in any
> mode but this."
>
> *John Stuart Mill*

In our media-intensive culture it is not difficult to find differing opinions. Thousands of newspapers and magazines and dozens of radio and television talk shows resound with differing points of view. The difficulty lies in deciding which opinion to agree with and which "experts" seem the most credible. The more inundated we become with differing opinions and claims, the more essential it is to hone critical reading and thinking skills to evaluate these ideas. Opposing Viewpoints books address this problem directly by presenting stimulating debates that can be used to enhance and teach these skills. The varied opinions contained in each book examine many different aspects of a single issue. While examining these conveniently edited opposing views, readers can develop critical thinking skills such as the ability to compare and contrast authors' credibility, facts, argumentation styles, use of persuasive techniques, and other stylistic tools. In short, the Opposing Viewpoints Series is an ideal way to attain the higher-level thinking and reading skills so essential in a culture of diverse and contradictory opinions.

In addition to providing a tool for critical thinking, Opposing Viewpoints books challenge readers to question their own strongly held opinions and assumptions. Most people form their opinions on the basis of upbringing, peer pressure, and personal, cultural, or professional bias. By reading carefully balanced opposing views, readers must directly confront new ideas as well as the opinions of those with whom they disagree. This is not to argue simplistically that everyone who reads opposing views will—or should—change his or her opinion. Instead, the series enhances readers' understanding of their own views by encouraging confrontation with opposing ideas. Careful examination of others' views can lead to the readers' understanding of the logical inconsistencies in their own opinions, perspective on why they hold an opinion, and the consideration of the possibility that their opinion requires further evaluation.

Evaluating Other Opinions

To ensure that this type of examination occurs, Opposing Viewpoints books present all types of opinions. Prominent spokespeople on different sides of each issue as well as well-known professionals from many disciplines challenge the reader. An additional goal of the series is to provide a forum for other, less known, or even unpopular viewpoints. The opinion of an ordinary person who has had to make the decision to cut off life support from a terminally ill relative, for example, may be just as valuable and provide just as much insight as a medical ethicist's professional opinion. The editors have two additional purposes in including these less known views. One, the editors encourage readers to respect others' opinions—even when not enhanced by professional credibility. It is only by reading or listening to and objectively evaluating others' ideas that one can determine whether they are worthy of consideration. Two, the inclusion of such viewpoints encourages the important critical thinking skill of objectively evaluating an author's credentials and bias. This evaluation will illuminate an author's reasons for taking a particular stance on an issue and will aid in readers' evaluation of the author's ideas.

It is our hope that these books will give readers a deeper understanding of the issues debated and an appreciation of the complexity of even seemingly simple issues when good and honest people disagree. This awareness is particularly important in a democratic society such as ours in which people enter into public debate to determine the common good. Those with whom one disagrees should not be regarded as enemies but rather as people whose views deserve careful examination and may shed light on one's own.

Thomas Jefferson once said that "difference of opinion leads to inquiry, and inquiry to truth." Jefferson, a broadly educated man, argued that "if a nation expects to be ignorant and free . . . it expects what never was and never will be." As individuals and as a nation, it is imperative that we consider the opinions of others and examine them with skill and discernment. The Opposing Viewpoints Series is intended to help readers achieve this goal.

David L. Bender and Bruno Leone,
Founders

Introduction

"I'm cured of HIV. I had HIV, but I don't
anymore."
> —Timothy Ray Brown, former
> HIV and leukemia patient

"This probably is a cure, but it comes at
a bit of a price."
> —Michael Saag, AIDS researcher
> at the University of Alabama at
> Birmingham

Timothy Ray Brown is the first documented person to be functionally cured of HIV, the human immunodeficiency virus. In February 2007, he received a bone marrow transplant for leukemia in Germany, after chemotherapy alone proved unsuccessful. His donor carried a rare inherited genetic mutation known as Delta 32. Present in 1 to 3 percent of Caucasians, it creates a resistance against HIV by blocking the receptors through which the virus enters cells. Also, Brown's immune system was wiped out with chemotherapy and radiation, known as ablation. Twenty months later without antiretroviral drugs, he showed no signs of the virus, and the findings were published in the *New England Journal of Medicine* in February 2009. Another report followed up on his condition in December 2010; Brown had a normal T-cell count, fending off assumptions that HIV was hiding in his body. His leukemia was also in remission.

He learned that he was HIV-positive in 1995, after a former partner came forward. Brown's physician, Gero Hütter, an oncologist and hematologist at Charité Medical University in Berlin, had the idea of searching for a donor who had Delta 32 in an attempt to cure Brown. "My first thought was, I'm wrong," he says. "There must be something I was missing."[1] Such a procedure had never been attempted before. The head of Hütter's unit and his associates were unsupportive. The patient himself had no expectations. "At that point, I wasn't that concerned about HIV, because I could keep taking medication,"[2] Brown maintains. After finding a match with double Delta 32—from both parents for near-total immunity—Hütter performed the dangerous transplant, which presents a 30 percent risk of death. Brown ceased taking antiretrovirals that day. After recovering, he was able to go back to work, ride his bicycle, and hit the gym. In February 2008, Brown's leukemia returned, and another transplant followed. It cured his cancer. Stem cells from the donor multiplied, fighting off HIV. "It works like scissors and cuts a piece of genetic information out of the DNA, and then closes the gap," Hütter explains. "Then every cell arising from this mother cell has this same mutation."[3] Tests of the highest sensitivity and various samples have purportedly demonstrated that the virus was eradicated from Brown's body. Nonetheless, complications and neurological damage occurred this time; his speech and ability to walk are somewhat impaired. Of course, he is grateful for the stunning turnout. "It's an incredible feeling—like a miracle," he says. "I had two lethal diseases and was able to get rid of both of them."[4]

But numerous reactions to Hütter's medical feat are critical and cautious. At a conference in December 2009, Robert Gallo, a researcher and the codiscoverer of HIV, dismissed it entirely. Miriam Falco, medical managing editor for CNN, contends that finding a transplant match for the vast majority of HIV/AIDS patients is impossible "because only 1 percent of Caucasians and zero percent of African Americans or Asians have this particular genetic mutation" and the expensive procedure is "not an option"[5] for millions infected with the virus. Jerome Zack, an HIV researcher at the University of California, Los Angeles, was "extremely excited" by the news, but questions "whether there's still some of that virus somewhere in the body that hasn't been sampled."[6]

Others herald its implications for HIV treatment. "Rather than any number of good ideas, we have a living, breathing human being who is proof of concept,"[7] proclaims Paula Cannon, an immunology and microbiology professor at the University of Southern California. Steven Deeks, who treats Brown and is a scientist at the AIDS Research Institute, believes the outcome to be unprecedented. "For the first time ever, something worked,"[8] Deeks declares. And Regan Hofmann, editor in chief of *Poz* magazine, suggests that "while the process Brown endured cannot be universally applied, Brown's case taught scientists much about how HIV works and how to produce a similar outcome without the risks of a stem cell transplant."[9]

The curing of Timothy Ray Brown is a potential breakthrough in gene therapy for HIV. Likewise, other measures to prevent the spread of the virus and manage the infection—such as the development of an HIV vaccine and use of highly active antiretroviral therapy (HAART)—offer hope, but no easy answers. *Opposing Viewpoints: AIDS* explores these and other issues in the following chapters: What Causes AIDS? What Is the Status of the Global AIDS Epidemic? How Can the Spread of AIDS Be Controlled? How Should AIDS Be Treated? The conflicting and impassioned arguments presented in this volume attest to the tumultuous decades of the pandemic.

Notes

1. Quoted in Tina Rosenberg, "The Man Who Had HIV and Now Does Not," *New York Magazine*, May 29, 2011. http://nymag.com.
2. Quoted in Rosenberg, "The Man Who Had HIV and Now Does Not."
3. Quoted in Kate Kelland, "An End to AIDS?," Reuters, June 1, 2011. www.reuters.com.
4. Quoted in Melissa Healy, "HIV Patient Timothy Brown Is the Boy Who Lived," *Los Angeles Times*, June 5, 2011. www.latimes.com.
5. Miriam Falco, "Not the Cure for AIDS," CNN, *The Chart* (blog), November 14, 2008. http://thechart.blogs.cnn.com.
6. Quoted in Rachel Rettner, "Cure for HIV Claimed, but Not Yet Proven," MSNBC My Health News Daily, December 15, 2010. www.msnbc.msn.com.
7. Quoted in Rosenberg, "The Man Who Had HIV and Now Does Not."

8. Quoted in *NAM HIV Treatment Update*, "Towards a Cure for All (Part One)," February 9, 2011. www.aidsmap.com.
9. Regan Hofmann, "Patient No More," *Poz*, June 2011. www.poz.com.

CHAPTER 1

What Causes AIDS?

Chapter Preface

In 1998, researcher David Ho and his colleagues announced that they discovered the earliest case of HIV. Taken in 1959, the viral sample was from a man who lived in the former Belgian Congo. According to them, HIV "evolved from a single introduction into the African population in a time frame not long before," and the virus resembled contemporary subtypes of HIV found across the globe. Furthermore, the researchers stated that it did not exist much earlier: "This finding also refutes the suggestion that HIV-1 subtype B infection was responsible for AIDS-like syndromes beginning in the 1930s in various European populations." Two years later, researcher Beatrice Hahn claimed that HIV appeared in 1930. She suggested that it became epidemic through "social disruption, enslavement, urbanization, prostitution, and other socio-behavioral changes not yet fully understood."

In 2008, evolutionary biologist Michael Worobey and his team published their findings that the virus appeared even earlier, developing at the turn of the twentieth century. They compared another viral sample—taken in 1960 from a woman who also lived in the former Belgian Congo—with dozens of others. Calculating how much HIV mutates over time, the team concluded that the virus must have emerged between 1884 and 1924, with a precise estimate of 1908. "The interpretation that HIV-1 was spreading among humans for 60 to 80 years before AIDS was recognised should come as no surprise," maintains genetics professor Paul Sharp. "If the epidemic grew roughly exponentially from only one or a few infected individuals around 1910 to the more than 55 million estimated to have been infected by 2007, there were probably only a few thousand HIV-infected individuals by 1960, all of them in central Africa," Sharp continued. Still, other theories for the origins of AIDS continue to abound. The authors in the following chapter present several of them, both within and outside mainstream science.

> *"The clinical and epidemiological evidence for the viral cause of AIDS is overwhelming."*

HIV Causes AIDS

Jonny Steinberg

Jonny Steinberg is a South African writer and author of Three Letter Plague: A Young Man's Journey Through a Great Epidemic. *In the following viewpoint, he blasts AIDS denialism, a movement claiming that HIV does not cause AIDS and even questioning the existence of the virus. Steinberg contends that staggering scientific and medical evidence proves that antiretroviral therapy (ART) halts the replication of HIV and onset of AIDS, thus proving the virus causes the disease. Researchers isolated the virus with people suffering from the disease in 1983, the author continues, and highly accurate tests demonstrate that HIV antibodies appear in the vast majority of AIDS cases. In the public, the confusion over the relationship between AIDS and HIV is due to a lack of education, he maintains.*

As you read, consider the following questions:

1. What is the "Lazarus effect," as described by Steinberg?
2. According to Steinberg, why do denialists argue that the

Jonny Steinberg, "The AIDS Denialists," *New Scientist*, June 20, 2009, pp. 32–36. Copyright © 2009 Reed Business Information–UK. All Rights Reserved. Distributed by Tribune Media Services.

scientific community cannot afford to admit that HIV
does not cause AIDS?

3. How does the author respond to the claim that HIV tests
are flawed?

On 27 December 2008, a well-heeled 52-year-old woman
died in a Los Angeles hospital. Her death certificate describes a body riddled with opportunistic infections typical of
the late stages of AIDS. Christine Maggiore had tested HIV positive 16 years earlier, but she had shunned ART, the antiretroviral
therapy that stops HIV replicating and prevents AIDS.

This was not the first time a death in Maggiore's family had
made headlines: five years earlier her 3-year-old daughter Eliza
Jane had died. The autopsy described a chronically ill little girl
who was underweight, under-height, and had encephalitis and
pneumonia—all AIDS-related. When pregnant, Maggiore had
again rejected ART and she had breastfed Eliza Jane, another
way of transmitting the virus.

Why, in 21st-century California, would a middle-class
woman and her young daughter die like this when there is tried-
and-tested treatment for their illness? The answer lies in a bizarre
medical conspiracy theory that says AIDS is not caused by HIV
infection.

It is tempting to dismiss the so-called AIDS denialism movement out of hand, but it has a strong internet presence, with
a plethora of websites and blogs that can mislead the unwary.
While the movement has lately suffered some significant blows
to its credibility, it has in the recent past wielded extraordinary
influence, especially in southern Africa, the centre of the world's
AIDS epidemic. "Denialism has been relegated to the fringes of
the internet, but it isn't of no consequence," says John Moore,
an immunologist at Weill Cornell Medical College, Ithaca, New
York, and one of the world's foremost AIDS researchers. "It can
still cost the lives of unsuspecting people."

The Origins of Denialism

The origins of the AIDS denialism movement can be traced back to 1987, four years after the discovery of HIV. Peter Duesberg was then a renowned researcher at the University of California, Berkeley, who had shown that some cancers were triggered by retroviruses. In March that year, Duesberg performed an about-face, publishing an article in which he questioned his original finding that retroviruses caused cancer, and also whether HIV (another retrovirus, although not one that he had studied) caused AIDS.

At the time, HIV science was in its infancy, and Duesberg was not the only mainstream scientist to speculate whether AIDS was actually caused by lifestyle factors such as taking drugs, for example. Indeed, *New Scientist* published Duesberg's manifesto of dissent in 1988.

"Duesberg did get laypeople's attention, and they, in turn, got him scientific attention," says University of California sociologist, Steven Epstein, author of *Impure Science*, a book on AIDS research. "Credibility was cycled back and forth."

As the clinical and epidemiological evidence linking HIV with AIDS accrued, however, support for denialism among mainstream scientists fell away. In the mid-1990s came the clincher. Cocktails of ART were found to halt the replication of HIV and reverse and prevent the development of AIDS. By the end of 1996, doctors in the west were witnessing the "Lazarus effect": AIDS patients who had been mortally ill were rising from their beds, putting on jackets and ties, and reporting for work.

By rights the denialism movement should have died out there and then. Yet it persisted. Not one of the denialists was a researcher studying AIDS or HIV—they simply critiqued the work of those who did. Much of the movement's output has been journalistic rather than scientific, spawning numerous articles, books, films (often self-published or self-produced), and lately, websites. Tellingly, most of the studies they cite are quite old, reflecting the fact that mainstream support has long since died out.

Ask what the denialists do believe, however, and there is no consensus. Some hark back to the early idea that AIDS in gay men is caused by amyl nitrite use; others say the cause is ART itself—although no one can explain why AIDS arose before ART was developed.

Some denialists accept that HIV may be present in those with AIDS, but claim it is just another opportunistic infection, rather than the cause. Others say, incredibly, that HIV has never been proven to exist at all.

Perhaps the most staggering of their beliefs, though, is that everyone else has got it so wrong. Denialists claim the scientific community cannot afford to admit their error because too many reputations and too many research grants are now at stake. Once ART was developed, the multibillion-dollar drugs industry had a vast investment at stake too.

It is certainly true that the scientific peer-review process can slow down the acceptance of new theories. And pharmaceutical companies hardly have a spotless record either. Yet the clinical and epidemiological evidence for the viral cause of AIDS is overwhelming, from virologists who see HIV under their microscopes, to doctors the world over who witness AIDS patients begin ART and make dramatic recoveries.

Denialism in the west continued to limp along, attracting a following of conspiracy theorists, attention seekers, peddlers of pseudoscience and HIV patients in denial. The movement's leaders vary in their credibility. Duesberg's most vocal supporter is David Rasnick, a former biochemist who makes much of his research background, as he once studied a group of enzymes called proteases. HIV possesses a protease enzyme, and protease inhibitors represent a key class of ART drugs. However Rasnick only worked on rat proteases, never on HIV's.

Then there is Henry Bauer, a retired chemistry and life sciences professor at Virginia State University in Petersburg, who edits the *Journal of Scientific Exploration*. This publishes research on such topics as alien abductions and telepathy. Before dabbling in virology, Bauer was a leading authority on the existence of the Loch Ness monster.

The Effects of Denialism

The effects of AIDS denialism in Africa are no joke, however. In 2000, as the movement was rapidly losing all credibility, South African president Thabo Mbeki asked some of the leading deni- alists to sit on an advisory council to guide his response to the epidemic. On their advice he did everything in his power to re- sist ART use in his country.

Mbeki felt the mainstream western view that AIDS was caused by a sexually transmitted infection reflected racist beliefs that Africans were promiscuous. Western science, Mbeki be- lieved, was blind to an obvious cause of immune deficiency in Africa: poverty.

It wouldn't be the first time. A century ago TB [tuberculosis] became endemic among black, but not white, South Africans, leaving western scientists flummoxed. Some pondered a genetic explanation, while overlooking the obvious—in white-ruled cit- ies black people lived in the crowded conditions that encourage the spread of TB. In other words, blacks were falling ill as a result of white domination. Mbeki argued that the same thing was hap- pening again. AIDS was simply a name for the diseases of poverty that had been legion in Africa since the days of colonial rule.

Mbeki was forced out last year [2008]—although not because of his denialism—and South Africa's new president, Jacob Zuma, supports ART. But immense damage has already been done. Last year, a study found that if Mbeki's government had provided HIV treatment, there would have been 365,000 fewer premature deaths in South Africa The legacy of Mbeki's denialism might still have an influence on the treatment decisions of many HIV- positive South Africans.

In Australia there is now the "Perth Group", led by Eleni Papadopulos-Eleopulos, whose science qualification is an un- dergraduate degree in nuclear physics. She appeared as an expert witness in 2006 for an Australian man appealing his conviction for failing to tell his sexual partners he was HIV-positive. Papadopulos-Eleopulos stood up in court and claimed that HIV does not exist. The man lost his case, however, with the judge noting that Papadopulos-Eleopulos had "no formal qualifications in medicine, virology, immunology, or any other medical disciplines. . . . Her opinions lack any credibility."

Along with Christine Maggiore's death, you might think that these events would significantly weaken the denialists' case. Yet it would be premature to predict the movement's demise.

Consider that in the US, two small surveys have shown startlingly high numbers of people—around 1 in 4—who question whether HIV causes AIDS. This probably reflects lack of education about the virus, rather than active denialism, since there is no evidence that people are seeking alternative AIDS treatment in large numbers. It does suggest, however, a troubling lack of communication between mainstream medicine and ordinary people. It is precisely such gaps in communication that internet quacks and conspiracy theorists can exploit.

Seth Kalichman, a psychologist at the University of Connecticut in Storrs, who carried out one of the surveys, has recently published *Denying AIDS*, a book about the movement. "My perception is that there is certainly a lot more mischief, like books and documentaries shown at film festivals," he says.

For some, no amount of evidence will overturn their entrenched beliefs. Maggiore blamed her daughter's death on an allergic reaction to antibiotics. For a long time she publicly cited her own good health as proof that HIV does not cause AIDS.

It is unpleasant to imagine what went through her mind last year as her own health worsened. She apparently continued to refuse the potentially lifesaving ART. Perhaps that is no surprise. To accept the drugs she had denied Eliza Jane would have been tantamount to accepting responsibility for her daughter's death.

And that's something that anyone would want to stay in denial about. . . .

The Myths of AIDS Denialism

MYTH: AIDS is not caused by HIV

Debunking: This is the biggie, of course. As long ago as 1983, researchers first isolated HIV from people with AIDS. By 1985, they had developed a test showing that the overwhelming majority of people with AIDS have antibodies to HIV in their blood. They also showed that people who test HIV-positive and initially appear healthy go on to develop AIDS the vast majority of the time unless they are treated.

Denialists often claim that HIV has never met "Koch's postulates"—a list of conditions that must be met to prove that a particular infectious agent causes a disease, drawn up by 19th-century German scientist Robert Koch. It is debatable how appropriate it is to focus on a set of principles devised for bacterial infections in a century when viruses had not yet been discovered. HIV does, however, meet Koch's postulates as long as they are not applied in a ridiculously stringent way:

Postulate 1: The germ must be found in every person with the disease. In 1993, the US Centers for Disease Control and Prevention in Atlanta, Georgia, reviewed 230,179 cases of AIDS-like illness. Only 47 people tested HIV-negative, less than 0.025 per cent.

Postulate 2: The germ must be isolated from someone who has the disease and then grown in pure culture. HIV has been isolated according to the most rigorous standards of modern virology. A small group of Australian scientists, the so-called Perth Group, claims that there is no proof that HIV exists. Then again, neither do the viruses causing influenza, smallpox, yellow fever, measles and many others, according to their bizarre criteria.

Postulate 3: The germ must cause the disease if given to a healthy person. Obviously no one is going to deliberately inject someone with HIV, but in three separate incidents, US labora-

HIV Hijacks the Immune System

HIV causes havoc in the immune system by selectively infecting the very cells that we rely on to protect us from viruses, specifically CD4/T-Helper lymphocytes. Think of your immune system as your body's army against disease and your CD4/T-Helper cells are that army's generals. These cells orchestrate the multiple components of the immune system to fight disease by sending signals to mount a coordinated immune response. HIV, like all viruses, consists of a small amount of genetic material protected by a protein coat or envelope. In the case of HIV and other retroviruses, the genetic material is RNA [ribonucleic acid].

Seth C. Kalichman, Denying AIDS:
Conspiracy Theories, Pseudo Science, and
Human Tragedy, *2009.*

tory workers accidentally exposed to purified HIV tested positive for that specific strain and later developed AIDS.

MYTH: Antiretroviral drugs are "poisons"

Debunking: It is true that antiretroviral therapies (ART) cause side effects in many. These range from nausea and strange dreams to ones that can be life-threatening if not competently managed, such as nerve damage. Some are temporary while others persist.

Side effects are less of a problem, however, for people in the west using the latest ART regimens. And whether the regimen is old or new, scores of clinical trials conducted on four continents have shown that the benefits far outweigh the risks. To take just one example, a study of 1255 patients over two years found that the death rate fell from 29 per cent per year to just under 9 per cent per year.

MYTH: HIV tests are flawed

Debunking: The two most common HIV tests, ELISA and western blot, both test for HIV antibodies. The ELISA test used to occasionally generate false positives, for example by cross-reacting to flu antibodies if someone had recently had a flu vaccine. However, this has not been a problem since the test was improved in the mid-1990s. Plus people are only diagnosed as HIV-positive after an ELISA test has been confirmed by the western blot, which is more expensive and complicated but more accurate. The result is that less than 1 in 1000 tests now produces a false positive.

MYTH: AIDS is caused by poverty or malnutrition

Debunking: This is often trotted out to explain the high toll of AIDS in Africa. In a study conducted in the Rakai district of Uganda, nearly 20,000 adults were followed for three years. The highest rate of HIV-related death was among the better educated and government employees, in other words, among the middle classes, rather than among the poor.

Even in South Africa, for several years the heartland of denialism, the figures refute the poverty myth. A count of death certificates in South Africa found that 57 per cent more people died in 2002 than in 1997. Poverty and malnutrition in South Africa were not increasing over this period—and the government itself says poverty actually fell.

MYTH: The lack of a widespread HIV epidemic in the west proves the orthodoxy is wrong

Debunking: In the early 1980s there were doom-laden predictions that HIV would spread from high-risk groups such as gay men and drug users to the general population. In sub-Saharan Africa, HIV is indeed rampant among heterosexuals, with rates among adults in South Africa, for example, as high as 18 per cent. Yet in the west and in many developing countries outside of Africa, HIV remains largely confined to certain groups.

Why HIV spreads through some populations and not others is highly contentious. One theory is that the strain of HIV common in Africa is more easily spread by vaginal sex, while the strains outside Africa are more easily spread by anal sex.

A different explanation is the "concurrency theory". It states that in African countries where there is a heterosexual HIV epidemic, it is more common for people to have two or more long-term sexual partners concurrently, which promotes the spread of the virus. Western heterosexuals, by contrast, are generally more likely to be serial monogamists. While they could have more partners over their lifetimes, those who contract HIV keep it trapped in a single relationship for months or years.

| "The proof that HIV cannot be the cause of AIDS is at hand in the technical literature."

HIV Does Not Cause AIDS

Henry Bauer

In the following viewpoint, Henry Bauer contends that HIV infection does not lead to AIDS. Bauer maintains that the presence of the virus does not correlate with the incidence of the disease and that the modes of HIV transmission have not been proven by studies or statistics. Furthermore, HIV has not been isolated in its pure form, Bauer continues, casting doubt on its existence and the credibility of testing. Bauer is professor emeritus of chemistry and science studies, dean emeritus of arts and sciences at Virginia Technical University, and author of The Origin, Persistence, and Failings of HIV/AIDS Theory.

As you read, consider the following questions:

1. In what ways do HIV and AIDS not correlate, as stated by Bauer?
2. How does Bauer support his claim that HIV is not transmitted sexually?
3. How did HIV become acknowledged as causing AIDS, according to the author?

"What everyone knows" is sometimes wrong. When it comes to science, including medical science, history might even suggest that what everyone knows at any given time turns out later to have been wrong to some degree: scientific understanding has progressed, after all, and it has often progressed by overturning earlier theories. But even as it's widely recognized that science has progressed, it's usually forgotten that this very progress has often meant superseding or rejecting earlier ideas. And the notion that a *contemporary* consensus might be wrong seems unbelievable to most people.

So the claim that HIV doesn't cause AIDS, when everyone knows that it does, is treated by the media, the public, and mainstream science as not worth attending to. And yet the proof that HIV cannot be the cause of AIDS is at hand in the technical literature, as well as in dozens of books aimed mainly at a general audience.

To consider that proof, it's necessary not only to specify that evidence but also to provide some assurance that good alternative explanations are available for what AIDS is and what HIV is. So those questions will be answered after outlining the reasons why the HIV = AIDS theory is wrong.

The Evidence

1. If HIV is the cause of AIDS, then there ought to be an obvious correlation between the presence of HIV and the incidence of AIDS. There isn't. HIV and AIDS are not correlated chronologically; they have changed differently over time. Nor are they correlated geographically: even from the very beginning, places of high HIV were not places of high AIDS. Furthermore, the relative impact on men and women is quite different—the male-to-female ratio for HIV has hardly changed over the years, while the ratio for AIDS has changed dramatically. So too with white and black Americans—the black-to-white ratio for HIV has hardly changed over the years, while the ratio for AIDS has changed dramatically.

If HIV causes AIDS, why then are there HIV-negative AIDS cases? Just how many is not known because after a substantial number had been reported, they were explained away as cases of a new disease, "idiopathic CD4 T-cell lymphopenia"—meaning deficiency of CD4 cells for no known reason, which is precisely the same definition as that of AIDS before the claimed discovery of HIV as cause of the immune deficiency.

There are also HIV-positive people who have remained AIDS-free for more than 20 years, the so-called "long-term non-progressors" or "elite controllers". The mainstream acknowledges this, but treats it as a mystery to be solved: why do some people have an uncanny ability to stave off either infection or, if infected, to stave off the harmful action of HIV? The mainstream view is that this is a rarity. However, since not every healthy person has been tested for HIV, it cannot be known with any certainty how many long-term non-progressors there actually are. Available data suggest that in the United States it might be as many as half of all people who would test HIV-positive.

2. The lack of correlation between HIV and AIDS numbers ought to be enough to settle the matter. But with so long and firmly entrenched a belief, there is no question of overkill by enumerating further strikes against HIV/AIDS theory. So it is worth noting that, whatever HIV may be, *it is not something infectious*:

- The estimated number of HIV-positive Americans has hovered around 1 million from the earliest time, the mid-1980s, to the present, whereas the incidence of infections increases and decreases.
- In any given group, the tendency to test HIV-positive varies with age, sex, and race in the same manner.

Infectious diseases do not display those regular trends. Infection is asserted to occur via blood, including transmission via dirty needles, and via mothers' milk, but chiefly through sexual activity. However:

- There are no authenticated cases of AIDS from accidental health-care-worker needle-sticks.
- More breastfeeding correlates with *less*, not more, incidence of "HIV-positive" among the babies.
- Sexual transmission of HIV has never been proven. The largest prospective study, in which discordant couples (one partner HIV-positive, the other negative) were followed over a period of years, could report no instances where the negative partner became positive.
- Incidence of HIV does not parallel that of known sexually transmitted infections (STIs); often rates of HIV went up as those of such STIs as gonorrhea or syphilis decreased, and *vice versa*.
- Use of condoms doesn't decrease the incidence of HIV-positive.
- A literally impossible level of sexual promiscuity is required to explain the prevalence of "HIV" in Africa—20–40% of adults having multiple sexual partners and changing them frequently.
- Pregnant women become HIV-positive more often than do non-pregnant women.

3. According to HIV/AIDS theory, the "viral load" determined by polymerase chain reaction (PCR) represents the amount of HIV present, which determines how rapidly the relevant immune-system-cells (CD4 T-cells) are killed off and therefore predicts the course of illness toward eventual death. However, there is no correlation between viral load and CD4 counts. The official Treatment Guidelines speak of three *separate* types of treatment failure: virologic, immunologic, and poor patient prognosis. If the theory were correct, then failure of one would bespeak failure of the others.

4. More than two decades of attempts to vaccinate against becoming HIV-positive have all failed. No satisfactory explanation

HIV Is Neutralized by Antibody Immunity

When a person tests "positive" to HIV, it means they carry antibodies to the virus. Which means that they have immunity. This is clear from the fact that there is so little virus to be found in HIV antibody positive people. The antibodies have done their job and the virus is well under control.

Health Education AIDS Liaison,
"10 Scientific Reasons Why HIV Cannot
Cause AIDS." www.healtoronto.com

for such failure has been offered, nor have the successive failures turned up clues to possible success.

5. More than two decades of attempts have failed to develop any microbicide that could inactivate HIV to prevent incidence of HIV-positive. Again, no satisfactory explanation for such failure has been offered. Microbicides containing anti-retroviral drugs, which purportedly kill HIV in vivo [within a living organism], have not been effective as preventive microbicides.

6. HIV/AIDS theory asserts that there is an average latent period of about 10 years between infection by HIV and signs of actual illness. The actual data reveal no sign of such a latent period. The median age at which people first test HIV-positive, the median age of people "living with AIDS" or "living with HIV," and the median age of people who die from "HIV disease" are all roughly the same: namely, the prime years of adulthood, 35–50.

What Is AIDS?

A huge complication is that the official definition of AIDS has been changed, moreover quite drastically, several times. The original, early-1980s, pre-HIV-discovery AIDS is not the same as present-day AIDS. A particularly portentous change in definition came in 1993.

It was around 1980 that, it's commonly said, doctors first noted that "young, previously healthy, gay men" were presenting with diseases formerly associated with immune suppression in transplant patients or in old people or babies with insufficiently competent immune systems. Given the concentration among gay men, the phenomenon was described as Gay Related Immune Deficiency (GRID). The predominant manifest illnesses were Kaposi's sarcoma (KS), purple blotches on skin and elsewhere; Pneumocystis carinii pneumonia (PCP); and candidiasis (thrush, yeast infections). GRID was soon renamed AIDS—Acquired Immune Deficiency Syndrome—to avoid placing the stigma for the disease solely on gay men.

A considerable body of evidence suggested that KS resulted from excessive exposure to nitrites, known as "poppers," which were in ubiquitous use in gay circles. A heavy strike against HIV/AIDS theory is that since the early 1990s KS has been attributed to a herpes virus (HHV-8 or KSHV), not to HIV, because there were many HIV-negative KS patients, many of whom had normal or even high immune-system cell-counts.

Initially, PCP had been thought to be a bacterial or parasitic infection, but it was later recognized that it is actually fungal, as is candidiasis. A plausible explanation for the rather sudden increase in those fungal infections among gay men, about a decade after Gay Liberation, indicts certain practices that can damage the intestinal microflora (beneficial bacteria) that protect against fungal infections in particular. Those practices include intensive rectal douching and excessive resort to antibiotics, sometimes for treatment of recurrent infections (gonorrhea, syphilis, herpes, and more) but sometimes even for prophylaxis. For descriptions of the unhealthy "fast-lane" lifestyle pursued by a small proportion of gay men, see for example Larry Kramer's novel *Faggots* and the documentary film *When Ocean Meets Sky*.

Moreover, it turns out that the first AIDS cases were not "young, previously healthy, gay men." Their average age was in the late 30s, they were anything but previously healthy, and their salient common characteristic was not that of being gay. It was their excessive use of recreational drugs, average age, and medical history that made a lifestyle explanation of AIDS highly plausible.

The lifestyle explanation had not been universally accepted, however, in particular not by virologists, who were at something of a loose end after a decade or two of unsuccessfully looking for human-cancer-causing viruses. HIV became acknowledged as the cause of AIDS following a press conference called by the Secretary for Health and Human Services, before any scientific publication on the matter, and the subsequent publications came nowhere near establishing the claim. For example, HIV was only found in two-thirds of all AIDS cases, and the patented test for HIV, which actually is for antibodies against HIV, turned out to give positive results even in many cases when the virus itself could not be detected by actual culture.

Still, the imprimatur of the Secretary for Health and Human Services and the attraction of grants from the National Institutes of Health, a subsidiary of the Department of Health and Human Services, brought virologists almost universally to research on HIV, and the Centers for Disease Control and Prevention (CDC) soon accepted the theory that HIV was the cause of AIDS. Thereafter, CDC progressively increased the number of illnesses that it regards as "AIDS-defining," just because some significant number of the patients tests HIV-positive, in tuberculosis, for example, or with cervical cancer. Those diseases are neither new nor opportunistically dependent on finding already damaged immune systems to attack, and so "AIDS" nowadays is an entirely different matter than the original GRID that was later re-named AIDS.

AIDS was originally a lifestyle phenomenon associated with particular damage to the intestinal flora. AIDS nowadays is any disease where an appreciable number of patients test HIV-positive.

What Is HIV?

Possibly the most incredible part of this story is the demonstrable fact that *HIV tests do not detect HIV*. An incredible part of that incredible story is that HIV has never been isolated in pure form, leaving ample room for the claim that HIV has never been proven to exist. A recent article reviews the relevant points:

- The original HIV test was based on selecting proteins that reacted strongly with something in the sera [body fluids] from AIDS patients, presumed to be antibodies to a presumed AIDS-causing virus.

- However, that these are HIV antibodies could only be confirmed with authentic virus, and no pure samples of virus have ever been prepared by isolation direct from an AIDS patient or after culturing.

- All later tests have been "validated" by demonstrating that they test positive when the original (Abbott Laboratories) test does. There is no "gold standard" for HIV tests and cannot be, since no pure virus has ever been prepared. The so-called confirmatory tests, typically the Western Blot but including the putative "viral load" measurements, are not confirmatory. As [researchers Stanley H.] Weiss & [Elliot P.] Cowan point out, they should be called "supplemental," not confirmatory.

- [Researcher] Rodney Richards has described how "antibody positive" came to be taken as proof of active infection, without the benefit of evidence to that effect.

- An authoritative description for detecting actual HIV *infection* makes plain that the tests in themselves are insufficient. In a population known to be at low risk—i.e., where the incidence of AIDS and presumably HIV is low (HIV ~ 0.1%)—a positive "HIV" test may be a *false* positive 5 out of 6 times if the test has a nominal specificity and sensitivity of 99.5%.

- In practice, the tests were calibrated to have high sensitivity, and therefore reduced specificity, because they were intended for and were approved only for screening blood supplies, where sensitivity matters a great deal but false positives mean only the discarding of some blood.

- When the tests are misused, as they currently are, to bespeak actual infection, considerable harm ensues to individuals who are told they are HIV-positive, and the psychological harm is compounded with physical harm if they receive antiretroviral drugs. Those drugs, widely called "life-saving," are seriously toxic; the Treatment Guidelines have acknowledged for some years that patients receiving antiretroviral treatment experience fewer AIDS events than such serious adverse *non-AIDS* events as organ failure (of heart, kidney, or liver) and cancer that are typical consequences of toxic medication.

So what is HIV?

It is a postulated but never isolated retrovirus. In practice, HIV means whatever is detected by an HIV test. But those tests are known to generate a high rate of false positives, especially in populations not evidently at risk; you can test HIV-positive after a flu vaccination, for example, and for dozens of other reasons. In any case, since rates of positive HIV tests do not correlate with incidence of AIDS, the question of what HIV tests really detect is moot as far as AIDS is concerned.

Tragic Consequences

The belief that HIV causes AIDS gained hold and then hegemony as a result of hasty actions based more on political than scientific considerations, and the unwarranted consensus has had tragic consequences. The conventional wisdom was taught that HIV inevitably leads to AIDS, that it is highly infectious, and that it is so life-threatening that even treatment with highly toxic medications represents a good compromise, even when it involves iatrogenic [physician induced] damage to pregnant women, the unborn, and the newly born. A perusal of the "side" effects of all the antiretroviral drugs, set out in the official Treatment Guidelines, makes the toxicity of these chemicals painfully obvious. AZT—nowadays usually called ZDV, zidovudine, brand name Retrovir—has been in use for more than two decades, virtually exclusively for the first decade. As its side effects the Treatment Guidelines list bone marrow suppression ("Onset: Few weeks to months"); gastrointestinal intolerance (immediate); liver damage (over months or years); disturbance of lipid metabolism (within weeks to months) with risk of diabetes; severe mitochondrial damage and lactic acidosis (within months); and Stevens-Johnson syndrome, or toxic epidermal necrosis (days to weeks). AZT was recently listed as a carcinogen in the State of California. Nevertheless, it still forms part of the "preferred" treatment regimen for pregnant women.

The mistaken belief that HIV causes AIDS has damaged the health of untold numbers of people around the world.

> "It is worth considering the possibility
> that new medical technologies
> introduced into Africa . . . sparked the
> global AIDS pandemic."

Bringing Modern Medicine to Africa May Have Caused AIDS

Helen Epstein

Helen Epstein is a writer, former AIDS vaccine researcher, and author of The Invisible Cure: Why We Are Losing the Fight Against AIDS in Africa. *In the following viewpoint Epstein theorizes that the introduction of modern medical advances in Africa led to the eruption of HIV and AIDS. A weak virus from monkeys may have infected hunters, she speculates, eventually evolving into a pathogenic virus as it passed through enough other humans, a phenomenon called "passaging." Epstein continues that the unsafe use of hypodermic needles, blood transfusions, and inoculation during the early 1900s contributed to serial passaging of the virus into HIV. Throughout history, in fact, new microbes have emerged in the wake of technological developments, she maintains.*

As you read, consider the following questions:

1. What is the "natural transfer" theory of HIV, as described

by Epstein?

2. What evidence about pygmy hunters does the author provide to support her assertion that natural transfer does not offer a complete answer to HIV's origins?

3. How would a blood transfusion in Africa have kickstarted HIV, according to Epstein?

Sometime in the early decades of the twentieth century—probably before 1930—five deadly retroviruses emerged from the African bush. Two of them were strains of HIV-2, and three of them were strains of HIV-1, one of which—known as HIV-1M—gave rise to the global AIDS pandemic. Many researchers theorize that there is a perfectly simple explanation for how this happened—that it resulted from what they call "natural transfer." Some thirty-six species of African monkeys and apes carry viruses—known as SIVs, for simian immunodeficiency viruses—that closely resemble HIV, and researchers speculate that the HIV viruses are really primate viruses that somehow jumped into human beings. HIV-1, the virus responsible for most cases of AIDS to date, came from a chimpanzee, and HIV-2, a less aggressive virus more common among West Africans, came from a monkey called the sooty mangabey.

According to the natural-transfer theory, AIDS is really an old disease, and viruses similar to HIV were always fairly common in a small number of forest-dwelling communities that hunted monkeys and apes for food. These viruses were passed to hunters when they cut their hands subduing or butchering prey, and chimp or monkey blood seeped into the wounds. In the past, most African people lived in isolated tribes, and this kept these viruses from spreading beyond the remote villages where the hunters lived. Then twentieth-century upheavals in African society changed everything. The far-flung regions of the continent were suddenly drawn together as never before by highways, labor migrations, and refugee movements. It is plausible that these highways for people were also highways for germs. At the same time, the trade in "bush meat" from wild animals caught in the forests of West and central Africa boomed. Today, some five million tons of antelope, snakes, gorillas, and elephants are eaten every year in this region. The roasted hands, skulls, and limbs of gorillas, chimps, and other primates are gruesomely displayed at food markets throughout West Africa. Many of these species carry SIV viruses, any one of which could mutate in the bloodstream of a careless hunter or butcher into a new strain of HIV.

During the past century, African wars of independence, the growth of African cities, new highways and truck routes, and the expansion of African mining industries drew unprecedented numbers of men out of the countryside. They left their families behind in the villages, and prostitution flourished wherever they went. Now the HIV viruses had many opportunities to escape from the bush, and every urban community, every truck stop and military barracks, was a breeding ground for HIV. All that was necessary for the virus to break out of the jungle was for a hunter or meat seller to cut his hand while butchering an infected chimp, and then for that hunter to migrate to a city or join an army and have sexual relations, perhaps in a brothel. The virus might then spread from the prostitute who had sex with the hunter to other customers, and then perhaps to other brothels visited by those customers, and then to yet more customers, and eventually to the wives of customers.

This is a plausible theory, even if there is something Victorian about it. During colonial times, Europeans fretted about the impact of urbanization on fragile native souls, and the transition to modernity was sometimes invoked to explain why Africans were so susceptible to tuberculosis, syphilis, and a range of other diseases. The natural-transfer theory implies that AIDS is the price Africans have paid for modern development, independence, war, urban drift, sexual license, and being cruel to chimps and monkeys.

A Genetic Shift

But there are other reasons to question whether the natural-transfer theory provides a complete explanation for the origin of HIV. In 1999, the British journalist Edward Hooper alleged that HIV leapt from apes to human beings during a laboratory accident in the Congo jungle during the 1950s, where American researchers were conducting polio experiments on chimps and monkeys. Very little evidence has been produced to support Hooper's theory, but his book—*The River: A Journey to the Source of HIV and AIDS*—is interesting less for its pursuit of the polio-HIV connection than for its skeptical treatment of the natural-transfer hypothesis.

As Hooper points out, early colonial and precolonial Africa was not all quiet villages and stable families. Since the sixteenth century, African wars have grown increasingly widespread and complicated, involving diverse tribes and European invaders. In the early nineteenth century, land disputes among rival chiefs in southern Africa ignited the "Wars of Wandering," named for the extensive migrations that followed. Prostitution flourished in the growing colonial cities of nineteenth-century Africa, but no one died of AIDS.

The slave trade, which reached deep into the interior, existed in Africa long before colonial times, and accelerated after the arrival of the Portuguese in the fifteenth century. Between 1700 and 1850 some twenty-one million Africans were enslaved, and at least nine million were marched to the coasts and shipped all over the world. During the two World Wars, African men were recruited as soldiers to fight in North Africa and the Middle East. These migrations did spread HTLV-1—a virus similar to HIV—that also seems to have come from chimpanzees, as well as malaria and yellow fever. So why not HIV?

Hooper also maintains that the AIDS epidemic must have been set off by something more than a hunter's wound. Africans have been killing and eating monkeys for at least fifty thousand years, and yet African and colonial doctors never saw anything like AIDS until the 1960s. HIV-1 is largely absent from the pygmy communities that still live in the forests of central Africa and hunt chimpanzees that carry viruses closely related to HIV-1. Pygmy hunters use rough tools to butcher their prey, so if the natural-transfer theory is correct, pygmies, if anyone, should be infected with HIV. However, the only HIV-positive pygmies identified to date are those who have had significant contact with larger towns and almost certainly picked up the virus through sexual inter-course. Pygmies do carry HTLV-1, which also spreads through blood and comes from chimpanzees, but not HIV.

It's possible that the monkey and chimp versions of HIV—or SIVs—are not harmful to human beings unless they undergo a genetic "shift" that transforms them into killers. In 2004, re-searchers from Johns Hopkins University analyzed blood samples from a thousand people living in the bush-meat-consuming ar-eas of West Africa, where HIV is thought to have emerged. They found several people with benign HIV-like viruses that closely resembled viruses from mandrills, mangabeys, and other exotic species that are commonly hunted or kept as pets. But these vi-ruses did not cause disease in those people, and did not spread to others.

In 1990, a laboratory worker became infected with a monkey SIV virus related to the one thought to have given rise to HIV-2 in West Africa. He was working with the blood of a macaque monkey that had been infected with an HIV-like virus from a sooty mangabey. The lab worker had been suffering from a case of poison ivy and the rubber lab gloves hurt his hands, so he didn't wear them. It is likely that he spilled something—blood or some other fluid with virus in it—on his hands and that the virus seeped in through the sores. The lab worker's immune sys-tem made antibodies against the virus, but the virus itself grew very slowly, and the lab worker never got sick. Similarly, sev-eral Africans, including two Liberian rubber-plantation work-ers and a woman who sold monkey meat at a market in Sierra Leone, were infected with the sooty mangabey virus thought to have given rise to HIV-2; but again the infections neither progressed to AIDS nor spread to others. This is virtually unheard of with real HIV infection, which never clears and almost always causes AIDS.

Perhaps Hooper is right. Perhaps something did happen in central Africa in the early twentieth century—and perhaps simultaneously in West Africa—to cause a very small number of previously harmless monkey and ape viruses to become deadly to human beings. Somehow they developed the ability to creep into semen and other secretions, and spread from person to person, and grow so rapidly in human blood that they were able to overwhelm the immune system and destroy it.

"Passaging" into a Pathogenic Virus

None of the AIDS researchers I spoke to share Hooper's belief that HIV came from a polio vaccine. Most assume that a small number of SIVs mutated by chance into human viruses and then spread widely across twentieth-century Africa, blown by the winds of change sweeping the continent, including urbanization, migration, and war. While I agreed that a single virus might mutate by chance into a killer and then be swept up by those winds, it still seemed odd that five viruses would do so in such a narrow space of time. After all, despite accelerated urbanization, the growth of prostitution and the bush-meat trade, and an endless series of civil wars and refugee crises, no new HIV viruses have emerged since the 1950s. Why not?

The reason may remain forever a mystery, but one hypothesis that Hooper pursues only briefly in *The River* intrigued me. A small number of scientists have suggested that the introduction of vaccination campaigns or possibly blood transfusions into Africa during the early twentieth century could have facilitated the evolution of HIV. While I was talking to Patricia Fultz, who studies HIV-like viruses in monkeys at the University of Alabama, she mentioned the work of Opendra Narayan, a virologist at the University of Kansas. I discovered that Narayan had actually succeeded in turning an apparently harmless monkey virus into a deadly killer in his own laboratory.

Narayan was working with a genetically engineered version of HIV known as SHIV—simian human immunodeficiency virus—which is used to infect lab monkeys. SHIV is a weak virus. It grows in monkeys but does not cause disease in those monkeys, and it is not passed to other monkeys through sex, biting, or other natural means. However, SHIV can be passed from one monkey to another in laboratories through blood transfusions or bone-marrow transplantation. If SHIV is transmitted artificially from one monkey to another and then another rapidly enough, through a process known as passaging, it can turn into a virus that spreads easily and causes a monkey version of AIDS.

"This has been known since [nineteenth-century French biologist Louis] Pasteur's time," Narayan told me. "If you take any virus and 'passage' it through a new species often enough, eventually you get a more pathogenic virus." To prove that this would work with SHIV, Narayan and his colleagues injected it into a monkey and waited for it to grow. Usually the monkey's immune system controls the virus and clears it, but this takes a month or so. During this time, the virus makes millions of copies of itself. As it does so, it mutates, so that not all the copies are identical to the original virus. After a few weeks Narayan took a small sample of virus from the monkey's bone marrow, where it was still reproducing, and injected it into another monkey. The viruses used to infect monkey number two would have been the most robust of all the mutants, having withstood attack by the immune system of monkey number one for the longest period of time. Thus Narayan was using natural selection to give the virus a head start in its battle with the second monkey's immune system. A few weeks later, Narayan took virus from the second monkey's bone marrow and injected it into a third monkey. The virus caused no disease in the first two monkeys, but it caused mild disease in the third monkey. But when, after a few more weeks, the third monkey's virus was passed to a fourth monkey, the virus caused AIDS in almost every subsequent monkey Narayan injected it into.

Something similar may have happened with HIV. If a hunter or monkey-meat butcher became infected with a harmless monkey virus and then shortly afterward passed it on to someone else, who then passed it on to someone else a few weeks later, it is possible that the monkey virus might have turned into HIV. Like Narayan's SHIV, the monkey virus might not have been able to cross from the hunter to other people by sex, but it just might have been able to cross to others through blood. This might have happened in the clinics and hospitals of early twentieth-century Africa.

Needles, Blood Transfusions, and AIDS

Many medical campaigns conducted around the time HIV first emerged involved what now seem like highly unsafe practices. During World War I, for example, six syringes were used to treat some ninety thousand people with sleeping sickness in the Belgian Congo. In 2000, the University of California anthropologist Jim Moore suggested that HIV might have undergone serial passaging during the smallpox campaigns carried out in West Africa during the early twentieth century, when thousands of people were inoculated with material from pox vesicles—blisters filled with weakened smallpox virus and with white blood cells, the primary home of HIV in the blood. These pox vesicles had been scraped from the arms of other people who had recently been inoculated themselves. Such arm-to-arm inoculation was common in Africa until World War I.

Another possibility is blood transfusion. Hypodermic needles were introduced in Africa in the early twentieth century, and blood banks were introduced later, probably after World War II. Perhaps a hunter or butcher carrying a benign monkey virus gave blood at a hospital. In Africa, people who receive transfusions sometimes donate blood themselves once they have recovered from their illness. Perhaps the person who received the hunter's blood became a donor himself a few weeks later and the virus was then transferred to a third person through another transfusion. This might have been enough to kick-start the virus. It might have evolved through such passaging so that it could grow vigorously in human cells and infect new people through means other than inoculation or blood transfusion. It might have become sexually transmissible, and deadly. I asked Dr. Narayan whether primate HIVs might have first adapted to human beings after being passaged through blood transfusions or inoculation, just as his SHIV adapted to monkeys through successive bone-marrow transfers. "Yes," he said, "that might have happened."

Such passaging events might be very rare. "We used to talk in terms of lightning rods," the AIDS researcher Preston Marx told Hooper. "You know—lightning can't strike twice unless there's a lightning rod. The lightning rod's the needle. That's why it struck twice in the same place—HIV-1 in central Africa and HIV-2 in West Africa."

Hooper dismisses Marx's hypothesis, and many scientists, although intrigued by it, remain skeptical. Although the theory is hard to prove, it is worth considering the possibility that new medical technologies introduced into Africa in the early twentieth century sparked the global AIDS pandemic. New diseases tend to emerge when our relationship to nature changes. If HIV entered human populations through such new medical technologies as needles, blood transfusions, or inoculation campaigns, it would not be the first time that a new microbe flourished in the wake of human development. Epidemics of polio emerged only in the nineteenth century with improvements in sanitation. Smallpox, brucellosis, tuberculosis, and anthrax probably jumped from cattle to people during the process of domestication. Likewise, influenza evolved from chicken and pig diseases; the common cold from a horse disease; and measles, rabies, and hydatid cysts from dog diseases. The prions that cause BSE [bovine spongiform encephalopathy, or mad cow disease] and its human cognate, new-variant Creutzfeldt-Jakob disease, or nv-CJD, emerged when producers began using the carcasses of sheep—some of which carried scrapie, a disease similar to BSE and CJD—to make feed for cattle, ordinarily a noncarnivorous species. More recent developments in intensive farming may have made possible the evolution and spread of yet more diseases, including West Nile virus and perhaps avian flu. Vaccinations, blood transfusions, animal farming, and sanitation have saved generations of human beings from malnutrition and disease, only for new plagues to emerge in their places.

| "AIDS erupted in the U.S. shortly after government-sponsored hepatitis B vaccine experiments . . . using gay men as guinea pigs."

AIDS Was Caused by Medical Research

Alan Cantwell

In the following viewpoint, Alan Cantwell claims that HIV is a human-made disease created by the government. Disputing that it "jumped species" from primates, Cantwell maintains that AIDS appeared exclusively in New York before its discovery in Africa. During the late 1970s and early 1980s, thousands of gay men were recruited as "guinea pigs" in hepatitis B vaccination trials, he claims, introducing a new retrovirus—HIV—and Karposi's sarcoma. He contends that these medical experiments are extensively documented but overlooked. The author is a retired dermatologist and author of AIDS and the Doctors of Death: An Inquiry into the Origin of the AIDS Epidemic *and* Queer Blood: The Secret AIDS Genocide Plot.

As you read, consider the following questions:

1. What makes gay men a "high risk" group, in Cantwell's opinion?

Alan Cantwell, "HIV-AIDS Was Created with the Use of Gay Men as Targets for Eugenic Experiments Suggests U.S. Doctor," *Canadian*, March 29, 2008. Copyright © 2009 by Alan Cantwell. All rights reserved. Reproduced by permission.

2. What speculation does the author offer about the presence of HIV and VS viruses among chimpanzees in Africa?

3. What was the fate of the gay men who participated in the hepatitis vaccine trials, according to Cantwell?

There is no doubt that AIDS erupted in the U.S. shortly after government-sponsored hepatitis B vaccine experiments (1978–1981) using gay men as guinea pigs. The epidemic was caused by the "introduction" of a new retrovirus (the human immunodeficiency virus, or HIV for short); and the introduction of a new herpes-8 virus, the virus that causes Kaposi's sarcoma, widely known as the "gay cancer" of AIDS. The taboo theory that AIDS is a man-made disease is largely based on research showing an intimate connection between government vaccine experiments and the outbreak of "the gay plague".

The widely accepted theory is that HIV/AIDS originated in a monkey or chimpanzee virus that "jumped species" in Africa. However, it is clear that the first AIDS cases were recorded in gay men in Manhattan in 1979, a few years before the epidemic was first noticed in Africa in 1982. It is now claimed that the human herpes-8 virus (also called the KS virus), discovered in 1994, also originated when a primate herpes virus jumped species in Africa. How two African species-jumping viruses ended up exclusively in gay men in Manhattan beginning in the late 1970s has never been satisfactorily explained.

Researchers who claim AIDS is a man-made disease believe it is much more likely that these two primate viruses were introduced and spread during the government's recruitment of thousands of male homosexuals beginning in 1974.

Large numbers of gay men in Manhattan donated blood for the experimental hepatitis B vaccine trial, which took place at the New York Blood Center [NYBC] in Manhattan in 1978. Extensive evidence supporting the man-made theory of AIDS is easily found on the Internet by Googling: man-made origin of

AIDS; and in my two books, "AIDS and the Doctors of Death" and "Queer Blood: The Secret AIDS Genocide Plot."

Government Interest in Health of Gays

Beginning in the mid-1970s, government scientists became interested in the health of gay men, particularly in the realm of sexually-transmitted diseases, and specifically in the sexual transmission of the hepatitis B virus. The early 1970s was a time when large numbers of gays came out of the closet and identified themselves as homosexuals at government-sponsored health clinics. Organizations such as the Gay Men's Health Project were formed at this time. Promiscuous gays were avidly sought as volunteers to test the efficacy of a newly-developed hepatitis B vaccine manufactured by Merck and the National Institutes of Health (NIH).

By 1977 over 13,000 Manhattan gays were screened to secure the final 1083 men who would serve as guinea pigs to test the hepatitis B vaccine. The vaccine was manufactured from the combined plasma of 30 highly selected gay men who carried the hepatitis B virus in their blood. Developed over a period of 65 weeks during 1977–1978 and tested for six months in chimpanzees (the primate in which HIV is thought to have originated), the first group of gay men were inoculated at the New York Blood Center in November 1978.

That same year a final cohort of 6875 homosexual men at the San Francisco City Clinic was assembled to study hepatitis B virus sexual transmission in that city. By the end of the decade gays in clinics in Los Angeles, Denver, Chicago, and St. Louis, also came under surveillance by the Centers for Disease Control. An additional 1402 volunteers were finally selected to participate in similar vaccine experiments in those cities beginning in March 1980.

Before 1978 there was no stored blood anywhere in the U.S. that tested positive for HIV or the KS virus. There were no cases of AIDS and no cases of "gay cancer" in young men.

The first cases of AIDS appeared shortly after the experiment began in Manhattan. In June 1981 the epidemic became official and was quickly labelled the "gay related immune deficiency syndrome", later known as AIDS.

The gay community was the most hated minority in America. After the experiments ended, the gay community was decimated by the "gay plague." In the first years of AIDS, the epidemic was largely ignored by the government (see Randy Shilts' bestseller, *And the Band Played On*) and the disease was blamed on gay anal sex, drugs, and promiscuity. Gays were immediately labelled "high risk."

In my view, what made gay men "high risk" was the fact that they were the exclusive volunteers for government medical experiments that undoubtedly put them at "high risk." The evidence for this conclusion is outlined in this report. Further evidence can be obtained from abstracts of scientific reports available on the Internet at the PubMed website of the National Library of Medicine.

The Gay Hepatitis B Experiments

The experimental hepatitis B vaccine injected into gays was unlike any other vaccine previously made. As stated, it was developed in chimpanzees and manufactured in a year-long process of sterilization and purification of the pooled blood of 30 gay men who were hepatitis B virus carriers.

The final group of 1083 selected for the first experiment at the Blood Center were inoculated from November 1978 until October 1979. At one point, there was great concern that the vaccine might be contaminated. According to June Goodfield's *Quest for the Killers*, p. 86, "This was no theoretical fear, contamination having been suspected in one batch made by the National Institutes of Health, though never in Merck's." Each gay man was given three inoculations of the vaccine over a period of three months. The vaccine proved successful, with 96% of the men developing protective antibodies against the hepatitis B virus.

It has been assumed by some that these men might have been already immunosuppressed due to promiscuity and venereal disease. Although the young men in the study were indeed "promiscuous" (this was a requirement for entrance into the study), they were in excellent health. Despite many previous sexual partners, these volunteers had never been infected with the hepatitis B virus, which was a requirement for participation in the experiment. Furthermore, the 96% success rate would not have been accomplished if the men were immunosuppressed, because such people often do not respond to the vaccine.

When [virologist] Robert Gallo's blood test for HIV became available in the mid-1980s, the New York Blood Center's stored gay blood specimens were re-examined. Most astonishing is the fact that 20% of the gay men who volunteered for the hepatitis B experiment in Manhattan were discovered to be HIV-positive in 1980 (one year before the AIDS epidemic became "official" in 1981). This signifies that Manhattan gays in 1980 had the highest incidence of HIV anywhere in the world, including Africa, the supposed birthplace of HIV and AIDS. In addition, we now know that one out of five gay men (20%) tested positive for the new KS herpes-8 virus in 1982 when stored blood samples from an AIDS trial in New York City were re-examined by epidemiologists at the NCI [National Cancer Institute] in 1999.

Never mentioned by AIDS historians is the fact that the New York Blood Center established a chimp virus laboratory for viral vaccine research in West Africa in 1974. One of the purposes of VILAB II, in Robertsfield, Liberia, was to develop the hepatitis B vaccine in chimps. The lab also prides itself by releasing "rehabilitated" (but virus-infected) chimps back into the wild, perhaps accounting for some of the ancestors of HIV and the KS virus found in the jungle by some government researchers.

In the decade before AIDS, the Virus Cancer Program (1968–1980), sponsored by the National Institutes of Health, attempted to prove that viruses caused human cancer. Ultimately the Program was unsuccessful in providing proof, yet it succeeded in building up the field of animal retrovirology, which led to a more complete understanding of how cancer-causing and immunosuppressive viruses in animals might cause disease in humans. The VCP was also the birthplace of genetic engineering, molecular biology, and the human genome project. As the VCP was winding down in the late 1970s, the gay experiments began in New York City.

The introduction of HIV and the KS herpes virus into gay men during this period (along with some "novel" and now-patented mycoplasmas discovered at the Armed Forces Institute of Pathology) miraculously revived the career of Robert Gallo and made him the most famous virologist in the world. And, of course, turned the "failure" of the VCP into a triumph by providing proof that these primate-derived viruses could cause disease in humans.

Fear of the Hepatitis B Vaccine

When AIDS began there were scattered reports in the medical journals questioning whether the "gay plague" might have its origin in the hepatitis B experiments. It was well-known in medical circles that the vaccine was made from the pooled plasma of gay men—and there was fear that the AIDS agent might be in the vaccine. As a result, when the hepatitis B commercial vaccine became available in July 1982, many people refused to be injected with it.

The fear of the vaccine was readily admitted by the CDC. Nevertheless, in detailed reports the CDC concluded that the vaccine was safe. Although it was clear the hepatitis B vaccine eliminated all "known" viruses, this obviously did not apply to "unknown" viruses at the time, such as HIV and the KS virus.

After HIV was discovered in 1984 some of the vaccine was retested and declared free of HIV. Of course, it was impossible to say whether the vaccine contained the KS virus, because this virus was undiscovered until 1994. I am unaware of any subsequent testing of the vaccine for this herpes KS virus.

Possible contamination problems with the hepatitis vaccine was the impetus that led [French virologist] Luc Montagnier to hunt for a virus in the new gay disease in the autumn of 1982. He began testing batches of human plasma for "reverse transcriptase activity" a biochemical sign indicating the possible presence of a retrovirus. Montagnier's research eventually led to the first discovery of the AIDS virus at the Pasteur Institute in Paris.

Although the CDC and the New York Blood Center claimed it was safe, many health professionals refused the hepatitis B vaccine. In 1985, only 23 out of 162 Rhode Island dentists agreed to take the vaccine because of concerns about AIDS. As late as 1990, 13 out of 14 black nurses at a university hospital refused to take the vaccine for the same reason.

Contaminated Vaccine

The purpose of the gay experiments was to test a vaccine that could immunize people against hepatitis B virus. Infection with this virus could lead to severe liver disease and sometimes to liver cancer. Ironically, an unprecedented explosion of cancer took place in male homosexuals after the experiment. Reports of the fate of these men attest to the fact that participating in the government's experiments was clearly injurious to the health of gay men.

Significantly, there were no reported blood specimens anywhere in the U.S. that were HIV-positive prior to the epidemic in 1979, except in the samples stored at the NYBC.

In a May 12, 1983, letter to the editor of *The New England Journal of Medicine*, Cladd Stevens (who supervised the NYBC experiment) wrote: "No cases have occurred in the vaccine recipients from populations at low risk of AIDS, and there is no excess incidence in the high-risk population." But this proved to be incorrect in later reports co-authored by Stevens.

In a 1985 report Cladd Stevens et al. claimed that seven men (out of 1083) were HIV-positive before they received either vaccine or placebo. If true, this indicates that HIV (and possibly the

KS virus) was already present in the blood of Manhattan homosexuals and could have contaminated the pooled blood of gays whose plasma was used to make the vaccine in 1977.

As stated previously, a 1986 report in JAMA [*Journal of the American Medical Association*] showed 20% of the men in the experiment were already infected with HIV by the end of 1981; and by 1984, more than 40% of the men were HIV-positive and doomed to death.

Another follow-up study of 8,906 gay men who donated blood for the hepatitis experiments in Manhattan was released in 1992. Statistical analysis of this group showed that mortality rates for men aged 25–44 began to rise in the 1980s, with AIDS the leading cause of death among young men in New York City. Remarkably, "The all-cause mortality in this cohort in 1988 was 24 times higher that the mortality rate in the cohort before the beginning of the AIDS epidemic."

Fate of the Guinea Pigs

Largely forgotten in AIDS history is the hepatitis B vaccine trial that also took place with 685 gay Dutch volunteers in Amsterdam between November 1980 and December 1981. Unlike the American vaccine makers, the Dutch researchers heated their experimental hepatitis B vaccine for added safety.

A 1986 report of the trial clearly states the AIDS virus "was not transmitted by the heat-inactivated hepatitis B vaccine." Of the 685 participants, five were already infected with HIV when the trial began. The researchers theorized that HIV entered the Dutch gay population at the end of the 1970s.

Another follow-up Dutch report of this trial in 1993 again suggests the efficacy of heating the vaccine for safety. (The experimental vaccine was not heated in the U.S. until after all the gay experiments were completed.) At the end of 1982, one year after the Dutch experiment had ended, only 7.5% of the Amsterdam men were infected. In contrast, 26.8% of the men in the New York experiment were HIV-positive; and a whopping 42.6% of the San Francisco men were HIV-positive. These statistics show-ing many men infected in the American trials in 1982 further prove that Cladd Stevens of the NYBC, and the CDC, were in-correct in declaring there was no excess incidence of AIDS in the "high-risk" gay male population.

The fate of all the men who participated in the hepatitis B vaccine trials in six U.S cities has never been revealed. However, it is likely from the statistics presented in JAMA in 1986 that many, if not most, of the men eventually died of AIDS. The ac-tual number of AIDS deaths has never been revealed, nor have the individual medical records been studied. Attempts to secure this information have been rebuffed by the Blood Center, due to the "confidential" nature of the experiment. . . .

Is AIDS a Human-Made Disease?

How did these two viruses of primate origin get into the gay male population to cause AIDS and a contagious form of cancer? AIDS experts blame monkeys and chimps in the African jungle. My research indicates it is much more likely these viruses were in-troduced during government-sponsored hepatitis B experiments using gays as unsuspecting guinea pigs. Extensive documenta-tion of past "secret medical experiments" by the government can be found on Google. A recent BBC news report (30 Nov 2004) uncovering unauthorized and dangerous HIV drug experiments on infants and children in New York City orphanages can be found by Googling: BBC + guinea pig kids.

Until proven otherwise, a "new" HIV retrovirus and a "new" KS virus could easily have been developed in a laboratory as part of the Virus Cancer Program. In the decade before AIDS it was common to transfer and adapt primate retroviruses and herpes viruses into human cells in genetic engineering experiments. Such viruses were deemed potential "candidate human viruses," as clearly stated in the annual progress reports of the VCP. For further details on the relationship of the VCP to the introduction of HIV, Google: virus cancer program + AIDS.

The connection between the hepatitis experiments and the AIDS epidemic was quickly dismissed by government authorities two decades ago. However, it is clear from a review of the scientific literature that the "gay plague" began immediately after the government experiments; and the experiments permanently damaged the health of the gay community, and led to continuing spread of HIV into the "general population."

Are we to believe that all this is merely a coincidence—and that AIDS in America resulted simply from two viruses jumping species in the African jungle? Or is the origin of HIV and AIDS—and the KS virus—related to secret medical research and covert human testing, as suggested here?

| "Most new cases of HIV result from
  sexual intercourse."

Sexual Intercourse
Spreads AIDS

Microbicide Trials Network

In the following viewpoint, the Microbicide Trials Network (MTN) states that sexual intercourse accounts for most new HIV infections. From 70 to 90 percent of all cases in women, MTN alleges, result from heterosexual intercourse; however, the network claims that the risk of HIV infection for unprotected receptive anal intercourse is twenty times greater than for unprotected vaginal intercourse. Additionally, breaks in tissue from trauma or sexually transmitted diseases increase the likelihood of infection, the author explains. Established in 2006, MTN is part of the National Institutes of Health.

As you read, consider the following questions:

1. Women account for what portion of all HIV infections, as stated by MTN?
2. How does anal intercourse represent a risk of HIV to women, as described by the author?

3. According to MTN, when is the risk of transmitting a
    newly acquired HIV infection the greatest?

Worldwide, the [AIDS] virus affects more than 33 million
people, more than two thirds of whom live in sub-Saharan
Africa. As a global crisis, HIV/AIDS shows few signs of slowing
down.

According to the most recent figures from UNAIDS and the
U.S. Centers for Disease Control:

• Approximately 2.7 million people were newly infected in
  2007—more than 7,400 every day. The number of new
  infections continues to outstrip advances in treatment:
  For every two people who begin treatment, five are newly
  infected.

• Globally, women account for half of all HIV infections, and
  in sub-Saharan Africa, women compose 60 percent of all
  infected adults. Young women are especially vulnerable. In
  southern Africa women aged 15 to 24 are at least three times
  more likely than their male peers to be infected with HIV.

• More than 2 million people died of AIDS-related illnesses
  in 2007; 1.5 million of these deaths were in sub-Saharan
  Africa.

• Between 2004 and 2007, there was a 26 percent increase
  in the estimated annual HIV/AIDS diagnoses among
  men who have sex with men (MSM) in the United States.
  MSM bear the burden of the epidemic in the U.S. and in
  other parts of the world, such as Europe, Latin America,
  Australia and New Zealand.

If the numbers don't tell the whole story, consider that behind
each number is a human face. Entire populations are at risk.

Prevention Is Essential

At the root of the epidemic is a formidable foe—a virus a million times smaller than the period at the end of this sentence

Factors That Influence Sexual Transmission of HIV

- Number of different sexual partners
- Likelihood that the sexual partner is infected (for example, behaviors such as injection drug use)
- Prevalence of HIV infection in the geographic area
- Number of sexual exposures with a HIV-infected person
- Status of rectal and vaginal mucosa (for example, whether it is dry or whether sexually transmitted infections are present)
- Infectiousness of the partner (this may include viral load and use of antiviral drugs)
- Use of barriers during sex (for example, proper use of latex condoms)
- Degree of risky sexual behaviors that are practiced

Felissa R. Lashley and Jerry D. Durham,
The Person with HIV/AIDS: Nursing
Perspectives, *2010.*

yet capable of laying a destructive swath nearly the size of the globe. Although newer drugs have dramatically improved both the quality of life and life expectancy of people with HIV, they aren't available to everyone needing them, and even for those who do have access to treatment, the drugs don't always work or they stop working over time. At the cellular level, HIV can play a skillful game of cat and mouse, mutating with frequency in order to evade detection by drug targets. In an attempt to keep HIV from winning in its own game, treatment strategies involve a combination of several antiviral medications that take aim at the virus from multiple directions.

Similarly, prevention efforts, if they are to be successful, will require building a global fortress, with several different defense strategies working in force. Among the approaches being considered are microbicides, substances designed to prevent the sexual transmission of HIV; pre-exposure prophylaxis (PrEP) with an oral antiretroviral (ARV) drug; use of ARVs to prevent mother-to-child transmission; vaccines; and behavior-focused strategies.

How Is HIV Transmitted?

Most new cases of HIV result from sexual intercourse between couples in which one partner is, knowingly or unknowingly, infected with HIV. In women, between 70 and 90 percent of all HIV infections are due to heterosexual intercourse. Moreover, women are twice as likely as their male partners to acquire HIV during sex, due in part to biological factors that make them more susceptible. Yet the risks of HIV transmission are the greatest for anal intercourse, particularly among men who have sex with men. There is increasing evidence that heterosexual women in both the developed and developing world also practice receptive anal intercourse. According to some estimates, the risk of HIV associated with unprotected anal sex is 20 times greater than with unprotected vaginal sex.

HIV is particular about the cells it infects. It targets T cells, a kind of immune system cell, and only T cells that have a specific molecule on its surface called a CD4 receptor. The receptor serves as a docking station where HIV parks before invading the cell. HIV then directs the cell's machinery to incorporate into its genetic blueprint the building blocks for the virus. By doing this, HIV ensures that with each cell division the virus multiplies as well.

HIV won't find many T cells on the surface of the vagina or rectum, but one thin layer below, these and other target cells lie in abundance. In the vagina, this layer, called the epithelium, creates a buffer zone that's a scant 40-cells deep. Merely a single-cell thick, the epithelium of the rectum is even more fragile. Just how HIV burrows down below the outer surface to reach its mark is not certain. Researchers propose there may be multiple mechanisms. Perhaps the virus hitches a ride with dendritic cells that straddle the two layers, having conveniently been captured by these cells as an "invader" to be turned over to T cells and other immune cells that would otherwise orchestrate an attack. Alternatively, maybe the virus uses more direct routes through breaks in the tissue caused by local trauma and/or a sexually transmitted infection (STI). A known risk factor for HIV among women, STIs may also enable HIV transmission and infection by signaling in armies of additional target cells as part of the immune response.

No matter what the underlying mechanism is, an infected cell that migrates to nearby lymph nodes is akin to someone with a highly contagious disease riding public transportation in a large metropolis. In lymph nodes, the virus is exposed to a host of new immune system cells that it can infect, each with the ability to spread the virus elsewhere in the body. Animal models have suggested that initial infection can occur within one hour of exposure, and dissemination of the virus, within 24 hours. Within three weeks of being newly infected, when individuals aren't likely to have symptoms or know they have HIV, the risk of transmitting HIV through sex is the greatest.

For its many challenges, preventing sexual transmission of HIV is not insurmountable. Compared to other sexually transmitted infections, getting HIV through sexual intercourse is a relatively inefficient process. In addition, the female genital tract is a relatively small anatomical area to protect. Researchers know that for any method to successfully prevent sexual transmission of HIV it must protect the surfaces most at risk; provide a sufficient therapeutic window and prevent migration of infected cells from the local vaginal or rectal tissue to regional lymph nodes.

| *"The risk of HIV transmission from any single [heterosexual] coital act is very low."*

Transmission of the AIDS Virus by Heterosexual Intercourse Is Negligible

James Chin

James Chin is an epidemiologist and author of The AIDS Pandemic: The Collision of Epidemiology with Political Correctness. *In the following viewpoint excerpted from* The AIDS Pandemic, *Chin refutes the claim that heterosexual HIV transmission will break into the general population without prevention efforts. According to the author, numerous studies show that the chance of infection from a single act of sexual intercourse is one in a thousand; moreover, Chin alleges, epidemic heterosexual HIV transmission cannot occur without high-risk sexual behaviors and very frequent sex partner exchange.*

As you read, consider the following questions:

1. What are the primary determinants of epidemic HIV infection, as reported by the author?

2. What is Chin's view of anal intercourse and HIV risk?
3. What vulnerable populations should be targeted in HIV prevention programs, in Chin's view?

I need to stress that my understanding of HIV transmission dynamics is not very different from most mainstream epidemiologists. The problem in accepting my conclusions and paradigm is that most AIDS activists do not want to acknowledge that epidemic HIV transmission requires the highest risk patterns and prevalence of HIV risk behaviors. These activists do not want to further stigmatize persons or population groups (MSM [men who have sex with men], IDU [intravenous drug users], FSW [female sex workers], etc.) who have such high levels of HIV risk behaviors and who are already marginalized. First and foremost, we have to be aware that . . . all published sex partner studies show the risk of HIV transmission from any single coital act is very low—about 1 per 1000 or less. By contrast, a pandemic influenza virus would be capable of *generalized* spread in any population because virtually all infants, children, and adults, young or old would be at moderate to high risk of infection to such an agent. However, HIV transmission requires the exchange of a significant amount of blood or sexual fluids. Thus, only a small percent of most general populations or "ordinary" persons would be at moderate to high risk of exposure to and infection with HIV.

Determinant Risk Behaviors

There is no question among infectious disease epidemiologists that the primary determinants of epidemic HIV transmission are risk behaviors that include having unprotected sex with *multiple* and *concurrent* sex partners and/or routinely sharing drug injecting equipment with other IDU. Epidemic HIV transmission has been documented only where the *highest levels* of such risk behaviors are present. Thus, it is only logical to conclude that in the absence of high HIV risk behaviors, epidemic transmission will not occur. What has been essentially ignored is the more important and relevant question: what are the major determinants of HIV risk behaviors? Most social activists do not hesitate to say that poverty and discrimination are the root causes of HIV risk behaviors. However, I don't know of a clear and simple answer to this question, since I consider it more likely that cultural, social, religious, and many other factors, including economic factors, all collectively play some role as determinants of sexual and IDU risk behaviors. Because there is no clear answer to what are the major determinants of HIV risk behaviors, many worthy social agendas have been hitched onto the AIDS program wagon. These social issues, such as poverty, discrimination, gender inequity, and lack of access to healthcare, are major problems that clearly hinder effective HIV prevention and treatment programs, but they are not the major determinants of epidemic HIV transmission!

Major Myths and Misconceptions

Below are what I consider to be the major myths or misconceptions about HIV epidemiology and transmission dynamics that continue to be used by UNAIDS [United Nations Joint Program on HIV/AIDS] and mainstream AIDS agencies to support the prevailing socially and politically correct, but epidemiologically incorrect, UNAIDS paradigm: *in the absence of aggressive prevention programs directed to the general population, especially youth, it is only a matter of time before epidemic heterosexual HIV transmission will break out in populations where HIV prevalence is low.*

Myth: Virtually everyone is at almost equal risk of infection with HIV.

The origin of this glorious myth derives from the initial short doubling times for reported AIDS cases in the early 1980s that led to the false conclusion that AIDS was caused by a highly infectious agent. Observations that HIV risk behaviors (sexual promiscuity in homosexual and heterosexual populations and routine sharing of injecting drug equipment) are present in virtually

Heterosexual AIDS Paranoia

One of the worst results of the heterosexual AIDS paranoia is homophobia. When we become really frightened, we tend to run from the people who make us face those fears. Now the media have been screaming at us that heterosexuals are not immune to a disease many heterosexuals thought could only occur to "them." For some heterosexuals, that reality threatens to obscure sexual differences, and evokes fears of death. So what do some heterosexuals do when they feel the fear of AIDS? They blame, hate, slander, or fear homosexuals.

With AIDS, we must understand the real, and yet quite limited, risks for heterosexuals, and intelligently channel our energy and federal dollars toward the groups that are really suffering the most.

H. Aaron Cohl, Are We Scaring Ourselves to Death? How Pessimism, Paranoia, and a Misguided Media Are Leading Us Toward Disaster, *1997.*

all countries throughout the world also led to the belief that HIV epidemics would eventually occur in all populations. However, it does not follow logically that the potential for extensive HIV epidemics in MSM, IDU, FSW and their clients is equally present in all populations and countries. Further, it is simply not possible for HIV to jump into any "general" population from these high risk groups to spread in epidemic fashion in "ordinary" people. There are no credible STD [sexually transmitted disease] experts who are concerned that syphilis—which is caused by a bacterial agent that is hundreds of times more infectious per coital contact than HIV—has the potential to sweep through general populations "like a hot knife through cold butter!"

The major characteristic of HIV as an infectious disease agent is that its risk of transmission is, in the absence of facilitating factors, very low for any single sex encounter. This characteristic of HIV is not something that AIDS programs or agencies usually include in their educational messages about HIV transmission. Both Jon Mann and Mike Merson [former and present head of the World Health Organization's Global Program on AIDS, respectively] specifically instructed me not to distribute a table I had prepared on the risk of HIV transmission by type of exposure since this table indicated that, in the absence of facilitating factors, the risk of HIV transmission per single coital act was about 1 per 1000 or lower. They were both aware that my table was accurate, but both believed that distributing this information to the public would be sending the public a mixed message about the risk of HIV transmission via unprotected sexual intercourse.

Risk Patterns Vary by Region

Aside from the low infectivity of HIV, the pattern and prevalence of HIV risk behaviors differ markedly from country to country.... The WHO/GPA [World Health Organization/Global Programme on AIDS] surveys of sexual knowledge, attitudes, behaviors, and practices (KABP) carried out in the late 1980s found that:

1. the pattern of sex partner exchange in SSA [sub-Saharan Africa] populations is mainly on a concurrent basis whereas in most developed countries, sex partner exchange is mainly serial, not concurrent and

2. a relatively large percent (up to 40 percent) of females in some SSA countries have sex outside of marriage, whereas less than 1 to 2 percent of Asian females report such behavior.

These findings, as well as the observation that the prevalence of multiple facilitating factors, that can greatly increase the risk of sexual HIV transmission, are more than 10 times higher in

SSA populations compared with most other populations, help explain why epidemic heterosexual HIV transmission has occurred in most SSA countries but not in most other populations. In the few Asian countries where epidemic heterosexual HIV transmission has been documented in FSW and their clients, this can be attributed to the large commercial sex networks that were present.

UNAIDS and most AIDS activists have either intentionally or out of honest ignorance ignored the fact that HIV is very difficult to transmit sexually. By refusing to accept the fact that HIV is very difficult to transmit sexually without the highest levels of sexual risk behaviors, AIDS programs have avoided labeling some populations as being more promiscuous than others. It is a much more socially and politically correct public health message to say that sexual promiscuity exists in all populations and thus the risk of epidemic heterosexual HIV transmission to the "general" public, or to "ordinary" people can be prevented only by aggressive ABC [Abstinence, Be Faithful, and Consistent Condom Use] programs directed at the general population, and especially to youth.

Predicted Epidemics Never Occurred

A parallel pandemic of AIDS "experts," most without any epidemiologic training, have used a variety of epidemic models to project large heterosexual epidemics in countries where HIV prevalence rates in the general population are still very low. These "experts" sound alarms that the "next waves" of HIV epidemics are imminent, or HIV is "on the brink" of jumping into the general population from existing foci in MSM and IDU populations. The "next waves" of HIV epidemics predicted for the general heterosexual populations in developed countries during the 1980s have never materialized. Most of these AIDS "experts" have given up sounding alarms about heterosexual HIV epidemics in developed countries and have turned their attention to large populous countries in Asia. For countries such as India and

China they project severe heterosexual HIV epidemics, if any sex outside of marital sex is permitted to occur, and education of the general public, especially youth, on how HIV is transmitted, are not aggressively implemented.

So-Called Bridge Populations

Myth: HIV "bridge" populations will invariably ignite heterosexual HIV epidemics

Another major misconception about HIV transmission dynamics is that infected bisexual males or infected IDU (male or female) serve as the "bridge" population for HIV entry into the general heterosexual population. What has been virtually ignored over the past two decades is that such "bridging" has and continues to occur from ... nonepidemic transmission between HIV-discordant couples, i.e., HIV transmission from an infected person (regardless of how infection was acquired) to his/her regular sex partner or partners. This is currently the predominant mode of HIV transmission throughout the world, but these are usually "bridges to nowhere." This is because epidemic heterosexual HIV transmission has not and cannot occur in any population without the presence of a very high risk pattern and frequency of sex partner exchange. In the absence of these latter factors there will not be significant spread within the general population. This is exactly what has happened following the hundreds of HIV epidemics that have been documented in MSM and IDU populations throughout the world since the early 1980s. This also happened with the many HIV-infected persons who traveled out of Africa during the 1960s and 1970s: there were probably hundreds or thousands of such "sparks" that introduced HIV into many populations but they did not start significant epidemic spread until such a "spark" was introduced into a gay bathhouse or an IDU "shooting gallery."

It should be noted that in SSA, where heterosexual HIV transmission has been so extensive, the majority of "general" populations, even in SSA countries with the highest HIV prevalence rates, are at low to no risk of acquiring HIV via sexual intercourse because they are monogamous or faithful to their spouses.

These aspects of HIV transmission dynamics were not fully understood during the late 1980s and early 1990s. In the USA and in most developed countries, where explosive HIV epidemics in MSM and IDU populations occurred during the early 1980s, the anticipated "next wave" of HIV epidemics did not materialize in any "general" heterosexual population. Michael Fumento accurately and in great detail documented this situation in his book *The Myth of Heterosexual AIDS*. However, he also seriously questioned the large and well documented heterosexual HIV epidemics in SSA and Thailand during this same time period.

Mainstream science and public health did not question these large heterosexual HIV epidemics but during this time period were at a loss to explain why epidemic heterosexual HIV transmission was so rampant in SSA and to a lesser extent in a few populations in the Caribbean and Asia and almost nonexistent in developed countries and most developing countries. Some of the initial theories were that: anal intercourse was more prevalent in African and Asian populations than was then believed and/or that poverty was a major determinant of high HIV prevalence. These myths or misconceptions about heterosexual HIV transmission continue to have staunch supporters. There has and continues to be some sort of fixation about anal intercourse that is also not warranted. There is nothing exceptional or mysterious about anal intercourse compared with vaginal intercourse with regard to the risk of HIV transmission. Anal intercourse results in a higher risk simply because of the greater likelihood of tissue trauma and thus more lesions in the fragile rectal epithelium compared to vaginal epithelium. However, there are multiple facilitating factors that can increase the amount of blood or sexual fluids that may be exchanged during vaginal intercourse and . . . these facilitating factors are highly prevalent in SSA populations compared to most other populations.

High-Risk Sex and AIDS Epidemics

Myth: All high HIV risk behaviors will result in HIV epidemics.

Until the mid-1990s, it was not fully realized that there are major differences in the pattern and size of commercial sex networks. It was believed, almost as a matter of faith, that once HIV was introduced into any commercial sex network, epidemic HIV transmission would inevitably ensue. I don't want to minimize the public health risk that epidemic HIV transmission can occur in virtually all commercial sex networks, but it should be realized that this risk can range from very low to very high. Fortunately, the risk has been very low in those networks where partner exchange rates are not the highest. AIDS denialists such as [Peter] Duesberg and his followers, who believe that sexual transmission of HIV is a myth, point to the many studies of female prostitutes in developed countries and in many developing countries that show either no HIV infections or only a few to support their theories.

Calculation of the annual probability of a FSW acquiring an HIV infection in a low HIV prevalence country indicates that large annual increases in HIV incidence and prevalence cannot be expected. According to these calculations, if there were several hundred thousand FSW in the Philippines, less than 100 might acquire an HIV infection each year because of sex work. These infected FSW can be expected to infect several male clients during an arbitrary work span of 10 years as a FSW. However, these numbers will be largely offset by the hundreds of AIDS deaths that can be expected annually from the thousands of prevalent infections in this very low HIV prevalence country. Since the early 1990s, sentinel surveillance in the Philippines has consistently found annual HIV prevalence in registered FSW to be about 1 per 1000. . . .

In any country, some pockets of very high sex partner exchange rates exist and they include: border areas with extensive population movement; extensive migration and/or travel away from stable social environments such as from rural to urban areas for employment; seasonal workers; migrant workers; military, sailors/merchant seamen; long distance truck drivers; large development or construction projects; etc. Primary HIV prevention programs need to be targeted to these vulnerable populations wherever they may be, regardless of whether the potential for epidemic heterosexual HIV transmission is considered low or high.

Periodical and Internet Sources Bibliography

The following articles have been selected to supplement the diverse views presented in this chapter.

Henry Bauer	"Suppression of Science Within Science," LewRockwell.com, December 17, 2009. www.lewrockwell.com.
Jeanne Bergman	"The Cult of HIV Denialism," *Achieve*, Spring 2010.
Contraceptive Technology Update	"Women at Risk for HIV: What Is on the Horizon?," May 1, 2010.
Seth Kalichman	"How to Spot an AIDS Denialist," *New Humanist*, November/December 2009.
Donald G. McNeil	"Precursor to HIV Was in Monkeys for Millenniums," *New York Times*, September 16, 2010.
Carol Midgley	"HIV and the Rise of Complacency," *Times* (London), June 15, 2010.
Martine Peeters et al.	"Origin of HIV/AIDS and Risk for Ongoing Zoonotic Transmissions from Nonhuman Primates to Humans," *HIV Therapy*, July 2010.
Rob Sharp	"Killer Syndrome: The AIDS Denialists," *Independent* (London), December 1, 2009.
Trenton Straub	"Thou Shalt Fear AIDS," *POZ*, September 2010.
Bob Unruh	"What If Some Other Behavior Cost 25 Million Lives?," WorldNetDaily, June 9, 2011. www.wnd.com.

CHAPTER 2

What Is the Status of the Global AIDS Epidemic?

Chapter Preface

On June 5, 1981, the *Morbidity and Mortality Weekly Report* identified five young gay men with *pneumocystis carinii*, a rare type of pneumonia attributed to a deteriorated immune system. A month later, a report surfaced that an additional fifty-four were stricken with Kaposi's sarcoma, a cancer unseen in their age group. Defying explanation and instilling fear, such events signaled the beginning of the AIDS era. "AIDS was a murderous, mysterious delinquent that emerged seemingly out of nowhere," maintain Melissa Healy and Thomas H. Maugh II, health writers for the *Los Angeles Times*. "Transmitted primarily through sexual activity and blood, it mowed down whole communities of young gay men, tore through a generation of intravenous drug users, and made orphans of millions of the world's children." In 1983, French scientists Luc Montagnier and Françoise Barre-Sinoussi isolated the retrovirus that causes the disease, the human immunodeficiency virus (HIV).

The thirtieth anniversary of AIDS was recognized in June 2011. By then, it had claimed nearly 30 million lives—615,000 in the United States. Currently, 34 million people worldwide live with the virus, including 1.2 million Americans. "As long as the AIDS virus threatens the health and lives of people here and around the globe, our work will continue to connect people to treatment, educate them about how to protect themselves, battle discrimination, and to keep the country focused on our collective fight against this pandemic," declares Kathleen Sebelius, US secretary for Health and Human Services. The scope of the pandemic, nevertheless, also draws skepticism. "[The drug] industry is making a lot of money, and if there was no HIV, there would be a lot of people who would lose business," alleges Prince Mangaliso Dlamini of Swaziland. "What is now happening is that they are making so much exaggeration about HIV/AIDS so that they can keep their businesses afloat." In the following chapter, the authors debate the global state of AIDS.

> "Unless rapid and effective action is taken . . . the size of the epidemic to come will dwarf the many deaths that have already occurred."

The Global AIDS Epidemic Is a Growing Threat

AVERT

Based in the United Kingdom, AVERT is an international AIDS and HIV charity. In the following viewpoint, AVERT highlights that 33.3 million people globally are infected with HIV, with 2.6 million new cases in 2009. Africa is experiencing the most severe HIV epidemic, and in nine countries one-tenth of adults (aged fifteen to forty-nine) are infected with HIV. AVERT draws attention to the fact that in Asia HIV infections are likely to increase due to three interrelated factors: an extensive sex trade, injecting-drug use, and transient populations moving within and through countries. Moreover, AVERT points out that funding for groups at high risk of becoming infected with HIV is in decline. High-income countries are characterized by growing complacency, with many providing international funding but failing to fully address HIV issues in their own countries.

As you read, consider the following questions:

1. What percentages of the adult population are HIV-

infected in Botswana and South Africa, as stated by
AVERT?

2. What statistics does the author provide for the AIDS epidemic in eastern Europe and Central Asia?

3. How has the prevalence of HIV changed in Argentina, according to AVERT?

When AIDS first started, no one could have predicted how
the epidemic would spread across the world and how
many millions of lives it would change. There was no real idea
what caused it and consequently no real idea how to protect
against it.

Now we know from bitter experience that HIV is the cause of
AIDS and that it can devastate families, communities and whole
continents. We have seen the epidemic knock decades off countries' national development, widen the gulf between rich and
poor nations and push already stigmatized groups closer to the
margins of society. We are living in an 'international' society, and
HIV has become the first truly 'international' epidemic, easily
crossing oceans and borders.

However, experience has also shown us that the right approaches, applied quickly enough with courage and resolve, can
and do result in lower national HIV infection rates and less suffering for those affected by the epidemic. We have learned that if a
country acts early enough, a national HIV crisis can be averted.

It has been noted that a country with a very high HIV prevalence will often see this eventually stabilise, and even decline. In
some cases this indicates, among other things, that people are
beginning to change risky behaviour patterns, because they have
seen and known people who have been killed by AIDS. It can
also indicate that a large number of people are dying of AIDS.

Already, more than twenty-five million people around the
world have died of AIDS-related diseases. In 2009, 2.6 million
people were newly infected with HIV, and 1.8 million men,

women and children lost their lives. 33.3 million people around the world are now living with HIV.

The Impact on Africa

It is in Africa, in some of the poorest countries in the world, that the impact of HIV has been most severe. At the end of 2009, there were 9 countries in Africa where more than one tenth of the adult population aged 15–49 was infected with HIV. In three countries, all in the southern cone of the continent, at least one adult in five is living with the virus. In Botswana, a shocking 24.8% of adults are now infected with HIV, while in South Africa, 17.8% are infected. With a total of around 5.6 million infected, South Africa has more people living with HIV than any other country.

Rates of HIV infection are still extremely high in sub-Saharan Africa, and an estimated 1.9 million people in this region became newly infected in 2009. This means that there are now an estimated 22.5 million Africans living with HIV/AIDS. In this part of the world, particularly, women are disproportionately at risk. As the rate of HIV infection in the general population rises, the same patterns of sexual risk result in more new infections simply because the chances of encountering an infected partner become higher.

Although West Africa is less affected by HIV infection, the prevalence in some large countries is creeping up. Côte d'Ivoire is already among the fourteen worst affected countries in the world, and in Nigeria around 3.3 million adults and children are infected with HIV.

Not all countries have experienced an increase in HIV prevalence. In Uganda the estimated prevalence fell to around 7% in 2001 from a peak of about 15% in the early 1990s, by 2009 prevalence was 6.5%. The decrease in HIV prevalence in the 1990s is thought in part to have resulted from strong prevention campaigns although it could also have been associated with a vast number of people dying from AIDS.

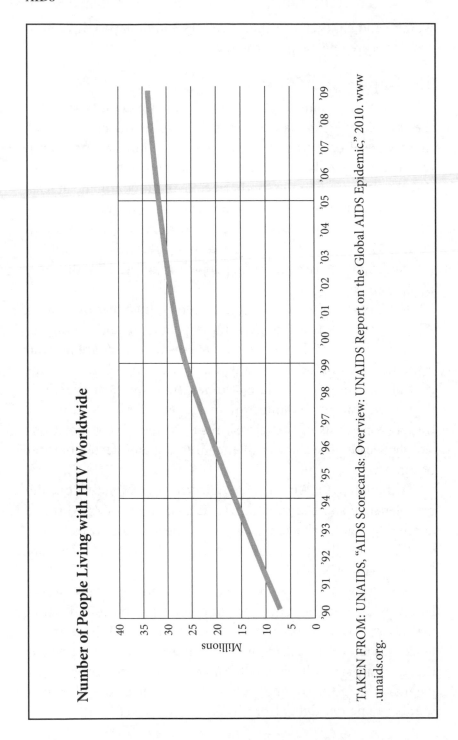

Number of People Living with HIV Worldwide

TAKEN FROM: UNAIDS, "AIDS Scorecards: Overview: UNAIDS Report on the Global AIDS Epidemic," 2010. www.unaids.org.

Although there was a rapid scale up of HIV treatment in sub-Saharan Africa in the first decade of the 21st century, under half of those in need of antiretroviral treatment in this part of the world were receiving it at the end of 2009.

It is widely thought that North Africa managed to sidestep the global AIDS epidemic—perhaps due to its strict rules governing sexual behaviour. However, the latest UNAIDS estimates indicate that 75,000 people in North Africa and the Middle East acquired an HIV infection in 2009, bringing the total number of people living with HIV/AIDS in the Middle East and North Africa to an estimated 460,000. AIDS killed a further 24,000 people in this region in 2009.

A Diverse Epidemic in Asia

The diversity of the AIDS epidemic is even greater in Asia than in Africa. The epidemic of AIDS in Asia appears to be of more recent origin, and many Asian countries lack accurate systems for monitoring the spread of HIV. Half of the world's population lives in Asia, so even small differences in the infection rates can mean huge increases in the absolute number of people infected.

The total number of people living with HIV in Asia is thought to be almost 4.9 million. Around half (2.4 million) of these were in India followed by China (740,000), Thailand (530,000) and Myanmar (240,000).

National adult prevalence is under 1% in all Asian countries except Thailand. However some of the countries in this region are very large and national averages may obscure serious epidemics in some smaller provinces and states.

In most Asian countries the epidemic is centred among particular high-risk groups, particularly men who have sex with men, injecting drug users, sex workers and their partners. However the epidemic has already begun to spread beyond these groups into the wider population. Some Asian countries, such as Thailand, have responded rapidly to the epidemic with extensive campaigns to educate the public and prevent the spread of HIV—and have succeeded in cutting prevalence. Other very populous regions, such as China, have only recently admitted that the spread of HIV threatens their populations, and as a result their prevention work is lagging behind the spread of the virus. Unless rapid and effective action is taken in this part of the world, then the size of the epidemic to come will dwarf the many deaths that have already occurred.

The epidemic in Asia has ample room for growth. The sex trade and the use of illicit drugs are extensive, and so are migration and mobility within and across borders. The fluidity in international markets has erupted into non-stop movement within countries and among countries, facilitating the spread of HIV. India, China, Thailand and Cambodia, to name only a few, have highly mobile populations within their borders, with people moving from state to state and from rural to urban areas.

Eastern Europe and Central Asia

The AIDS epidemic in Eastern Europe and Central Asia is rapidly increasing. In 2009, some 1.4 million people were living with HIV, compared to 900,000 in 2001. AIDS claimed an estimated 76,000 lives during 2009, over four times 2001's figure.

In any country where rates of injecting drug use and needle sharing are high, a fresh outbreak of HIV is liable to occur at any time. This is especially true of the countries in Eastern Europe where the HIV epidemics are still young and have so far spared some cities and sub-populations. Heroin smuggled into the West crosses through a number of Eastern European countries, and its path is marked by a high concentration of injecting drug users, and a high HIV prevalence.

The Russian Federation, Ukraine, and the Baltic states (Estonia, Latvia, and Lithuania) are the worst affected, although HIV continues to spread in Belarus, Moldova and Kazakhstan, and more recent epidemics are emerging in Kyrgyzstan and Uzbekistan. An estimated 980,000 HIV-infected people were living in the Russian Federation at the end of 2009. However, as reporting of HIV cases in many areas of Russia is at best patchy, it is difficult to determine a precise figure. The epidemic in Eastern Europe is primarily driven by injecting drug use, and the criminalisation of this practice makes it difficult to gain an accurate picture of the proportion of drug users who are living with HIV.

AIDS Ravages the Caribbean

HIV is ravaging the populations of several Caribbean island states. Indeed some have worse epidemics than any other country in the world outside sub-Saharan Africa. In the most affected countries of the Caribbean, the spread of HIV infection is driven by unprotected sex between men and women, although infections associated with injecting drug use are common in some places, such as Puerto Rico.

The Bahamas is the worst affected nation in the region, with a prevalence of 3%. Haiti, where the spread of HIV may well have been fuelled by decades of poor governance and conflict, has also been hard hit by the AIDS epidemic. An estimated 1.9% of Haitian adults were living with HIV at the end of 2009, though rates vary considerably between regions. HIV transmission in Haiti is overwhelmingly heterosexual, and both infection and death are concentrated in young adults. Many tens of thousands of Haitian children have lost one or both of their parents to AIDS. Among pregnant women in urban areas, HIV prevalence appears to have fallen by half between the mid-1990s and 2003–2004. Probably much of this decline is due to an increase in the AIDS death rate, though behaviour change might also have played a part. There is still an urgent need for intensified prevention efforts in Haiti.

AIDS is now high on the agendas of many governments in this region, as they are beginning to notice the significant impact of the epidemic on their medical systems and labour force. Cuba's comprehensive testing and prevention programmes have helped to keep its HIV infection rate below 0.1%, and the country provides free AIDS treatment to all those in need. In 2002, the Pan Caribbean Partnership Against HIV/AIDS (PANCAP) signed a deal with six pharmaceutical companies which lowered prices for ARVs [antiretroviral drugs] and led to wider access to treatment. In 2009, 48% of those in need of treatment in the Caribbean were receiving it.

Latin America Shows Diverse Epidemics

Around 1.4 million people were living with HIV in Latin America at the end of 2009. During that year, around 58,000 people died of AIDS and an estimated 92,000 were newly infected. The HIV epidemics in Latin America are highly diverse, and are fuelled by varying combinations of unsafe sex (both between men, and between men and women) and injecting drug use. In nearly all countries, the highest rates of HIV infection are found among men who have sex with men, and the second highest rates are found among female sex workers.

The Central American nation of Belize has a well-established epidemic, with the adult HIV prevalence above 2%. The virus is mainly spread through unprotected sex, particularly commercial sex and sex between men.

Commercial sex and sex between men are the major drivers of smaller epidemics elsewhere in Central America, where national HIV prevalence varies between 0.2% and 1%. Men who become infected via these routes are likely to pass the virus on to their wives and girlfriends.

Brazil had an adult HIV prevalence between 0.3 and 0.6% at the end of 2009, but, because of its large overall population, this country accounts for nearly half of all people living with HIV in Latin America. In Brazil, heterosexual transmission, injecting drug use and sex between men account for roughly equal numbers of infections.

HIV in Argentina was initially seen as a disease of male injecting drug users and men who have sex with men. Now the virus is spread mostly through heterosexual intercourse, and is affecting a rising number of women. The other Andean countries are currently among those least affected by HIV, although risky behaviour has been recorded in many groups.

One of the defining features of the Latin American epidemic is that several populous countries, including Argentina, Brazil and Mexico, are attempting to provide antiretroviral therapy to all those who need it. The governments of these countries have encouraged local pharmaceutical manufacturers to produce cheaper generic copies of patented medicines. This allows them to distribute drugs to a much greater proportion of their population that they would otherwise be able to help.

Treatment coverage still varies widely, but these efforts are having a definite impact. While they are improving both the length and the quality of people's lives, they are also increasing the proportion of people living with HIV, and thus HIV prevalence figures. Some concern has been voiced over the harm that HIV prevention activities may suffer if much effort and money is devoted to providing treatment.

High-Income Countries

In high-income nations, HIV infections have historically been concentrated principally among injecting drug users and gay men. These groups are still at high risk, but heterosexual intercourse accounts for a growing proportion of cases. In the United States, a quarter of people diagnosed with AIDS in 2008 were female, and three quarters of these women were infected as a result of heterosexual sex. In several countries in Western Europe, including the United Kingdom, heterosexual contact is the most frequent cause of newly diagnosed infections.

Very early in the epidemic, once information and services for prevention had been made available to most of the population, the level of unprotected sex fell in many countries and the demand rose for reproductive health services, HIV counselling and testing and other preventive services.

Prevention work in high-income countries has declined, and sexual-health education in schools is still not universally guaranteed, in spite of the fact that the risks of HIV are well-known to governments. Political factors have been allowed to control the HIV prevention work that is done, and politicians are commonly keen to avoid talking about any sexual issues. Furthermore, it is very hard to show that a number of people are not HIV positive who otherwise would be—and politicians like the electorate to see results.

Among gay men, the virus had spread widely before it was even identified and had established a firm grip on the population by the early 1980s. With massive early prevention campaigns targeted at gay communities, risk behaviour was substantially reduced and the rate of new infections dropped significantly during the mid- and late 1980s. Recent information suggests, however, that risky behaviour may be increasing again in some communities. People think that the danger is over because of lack of media coverage of the issues around HIV and AIDS—and many new infections continue to occur.

Some communities and countries have initiated aggressive HIV prevention efforts, particularly among high-risk groups such as injecting drug users. But in many places the political cost of implementing needle exchange and other prevention programmes has been considered too high for them to be started or maintained.

Many high-income countries suffer from the belief that HIV is something that affects other people, not their own populations. On a national level, this belief prevents policy makers and budget setters from seeing the epidemic on their own doorsteps, looking instead to the situation in areas such as Africa. Some high-income countries fund medication provision for low-income countries whilst failing to provide medicines for their own citizens who have AIDS. For example, many people cannot afford HIV treatment in America.

Where Does It Go from Here?

Spending. Significant money is being spent particularly on providing treatment for HIV/AIDS, but there are large numbers of

The Need to Be Seen

Some experts say that tallying HIV cases is not as important as finding the resources to fight the disease. But to researchers who drive AIDS policies, differences in infection rates are not merely academic. Programmes deemed successful are urged on and funded lavishly by international donors, often to the exclusion of other projects. Hence the need to be seen to be succeeding.

Gatonye Gathura, Daily Nation,
July 6, 2006.

people still needing treatment and funding from many organisations, including the Global Fund and PEPFAR [US President's Emergency Plan for AIDS Relief], is either being reduced or at best is staying the same.

Prevention and education. HIV education has already been proved to be effective and necessary, both for people who are not infected with HIV—to enable them to protect themselves from HIV—and for people who are HIV positive—to help them to live with the virus. There is a huge wealth of educational resources available around the world, and yet in many places people still lack the knowledge they need to protect themselves.

HIV and AIDS prevention is possible, but to avoid HIV infection people need more than just factual information. People need empowerment to negotiate safe and responsible sexual relationships; gender inequalities must be confronted; and those who choose to have sex need access to condoms. Needle exchanges should be encouraged, as they have proven highly effective at preventing HIV transmission among injecting drug users.

Medication. Antiretroviral AIDS medication is now being distributed in high prevalence countries, but there must be increasing access to HIV treatment if millions of more deaths are to be avoided. Along with the actual availability of drugs, one of the greatest challenges is a shortage of health workers to carry out HIV tests, administer the medicines, and teach people how to use them.

HIV is recognised as a global threat, and funding and resources for the HIV epidemic have increased significantly since the 1990s. However, the global economic recession has led to declining financial commitment and successful treatment regimes have also been shown to lead to complacency about HIV prevention. Much has been achieved but the momentum must be maintained or the hard-won achievements of the past two decades risk being reversed.

> "Exaggerated claims for the scale of
> the HIV epidemic (and the risks of
> wider spread) . . . enable authorities to
> claim the credit for subsequently lower
> figures."

The Global AIDS Epidemic Is Exaggerated

Michael Fitzpatrick

In the following viewpoint, Michael Fitzpatrick argues that advocacy organizations and government agencies exaggerate the scale of the AIDS epidemic. According to him, the prevalence and incidence is low in most parts of the world, and former industry insiders claim that statistics are manipulated to perpetuate the politically correct myth that all populations are at risk of HIV and AIDS. Fitzpatrick insists that such efforts to change the whole public's sexual behavior are misguided and wasteful, ignoring the real problem of HIV transmission among gay men, drug users, and prostitutes. Fitzpatrick is author of The Tyranny of Health: Doctors and the Regulation of Lifestyle *and* The Truth About the AIDS Panic.

As you read, consider the following questions:

1. What positions did James Chin and Elizabeth Pisani

Michael Fitzpatrick, "AIDS Epidemic? It Was a 'Glorious Myth,'" *spiked*, September 5, 2008. Copyright © 2008 by spiked Ltd. All rights reserved. Reproduced by permission.

hold before challenging the AIDS epidemic, according to Fitzpatrick?

2. What was clear by the late 1980s about HIV transmission and heterosexual sex, as stated by the author?

3. By how much has the actual prevalence of HIV in sub-Saharan African and the Caribbean been overstated, as argued by Fitzpatrick?

There is a widely accepted view that Britain was saved from an explosive epidemic of heterosexual AIDS in the late 1980s by a bold campaign initiated by gay activists and radical doctors and subsequently endorsed by the government and the mass media.

According to advocates of this view, we owe our low rates of HIV infection today largely to the success of initiatives such as the 'Don't Die of Ignorance' leaflet distributed to 23 million households and the scary 'Tombstones and Icebergs' television and cinema adverts (though they are always quick to add that we must maintain vigilance and guard against complacency).

A "Glorious Myth"

Now former AIDS industry insiders are challenging the imminent heterosexual plague story and many of the other scare stories of the international AIDS panic. James Chin, author of *The AIDS Pandemic: The Collision of Epidemiology with Political Correctness*, is a veteran public health epidemiologist who worked in the World Health Organisation's Global Programme on AIDS in the late 1980s and early 1990s. Elizabeth Pisani, a journalist turned epidemiologist and author of *The Wisdom of Whores: Bureaucrats, Brothels and the Business of AIDS*, spent most of the past decade working under the auspices of UNAIDS [United Nations Joint Program on HIV/AIDS], which took over the global crusade against HIV in 1996. Once prominent advocates of the familiar doomsday scenarios, both have now turned whistleblowers on their former colleagues in the AIDS bureaucracy, a 'byzantine' world, according to Pisani, in which 'money eclipses truth'.

For Chin, the British AIDS story is an example of a 'glorious myth'—a tale that is 'gloriously or nobly false', but told 'for a good cause'. He claims that government and international agencies, and AIDS advocacy organisations, 'have distorted HIV epidemiology in order to perpetuate the myth of the great potential for HIV epidemics to spread into "general" populations'. In particular, he alleges, HIV/AIDS 'estimates and projections are "cooked" or made up'.

While Pisani disputes Chin's claim that UNAIDS epidemiologists deliberately overestimated the epidemic, she admits to what she describes as 'beating up' the figures, insisting— unconvincingly—that there is a 'huge difference' between 'making it up (plain old lying) and beating it up'. Pisani freely acknowledges her role in manipulating statistics to maximise their scare value, and breezily dismisses the 'everyone-is-at-risk nonsense' of the British 'Don't Die of Ignorance' campaign.

Chin's book offers a comprehensive exposure of the hollowness of the claims of the AIDS bureaucracy for the efficacy of their preventive campaigns. He provides numerous examples of how exaggerated claims for the scale of the HIV epidemic (and the risks of wider spread) in different countries and contexts enable authorities to claim the credit for subsequently lower figures, as they 'ride to glory' on curves showing declining incidence. As he argues, 'HIV prevalence is low in most populations throughout the world and can be expected to remain low, not because of effective HIV prevention programmes, but because . . . the vast majority of the world's populations do not have sufficient HIV risk behaviours to sustain epidemic HIV transmission'.

By the late 1980s, it was already clear that, given the very low prevalence of HIV, the difficulty of transmitting HIV through heterosexual sex and the stable character of sexual relationships (even those having multiple partners tend to favour serial monogamy), an explosive HIV epidemic in Britain, of the sort that occurred in relatively small networks of gay men and drug users, was highly improbable, as [commentator] Don Milligan and I argued in 1987.

As both Chin and Pisani indicate, high rates of heterosexually spread HIV infection remain the exceptional feature of sub-Saharan Africa (and parts of the Caribbean) where a particular pattern of concurrent networks of sexual partners together with high rates of other sexually transmitted infections facilitated an AIDS epidemic. Though this has had a devastating impact on many communities, Chin suggests that HIV prevalence in sub-Saharan Africa and the Caribbean has been overestimated by about 50 per cent. The good news is that, contrary to the doom-mongering of the AIDS bureaucracy, the rising annual global HIV incidence peaked in the late 1990s and the AIDS pandemic has now passed its peak.

Most significantly, the sub-Saharan pattern has not been replicated in Europe or North America, or even in Asia or Latin America, though there have been localised epidemics associated with gay men, drug users and prostitution, most recently in South-East Asia and Eastern Europe.

The "Everyone-Is-at-Risk" Nonsense

Many commentators now acknowledge the gross exaggerations and scaremongering of the AIDS bureaucracy. It is clear that HIV has remained largely confined to people following recognised high-risk behaviours, rather than being, in the mantra of the AIDS bureaucracy, a condition of poverty, gender inequality and under-development. Yet they also accept the argument, characterised by Chin as 'political correctness', that it is better to try to terrify the entire population with the spectre of an AIDS epidemic than it is to risk stigmatising the gays and junkies, ladyboys and whores who feature prominently in Pisani's colourful account.

For Chin and Pisani, the main problem of the mendacity of the AIDS bureaucracy is that it leads to misdirected, ineffective and wasteful campaigns to change the sexual behaviour of the entire population, while the real problems of HIV transmission through high-risk networks are neglected. To deal with these problems, both favour a return to traditional public health methods of containing sexually transmitted infections through aggressive testing, contact tracing and treatment of carriers of HIV. Whereas the gay activists who influenced the early approach of the AIDS bureaucracy favoured anonymous and voluntary testing, our whistleblowers now recommend a more coercive approach, in relation to both diagnosis and treatment.

Pisani reminds readers that 'public health is inherently a somewhat fascist discipline' (for example, quarantine restrictions have an inescapably authoritarian character) and enthusiastically endorses the AIDS policies of the Thai military authorities and the Chinese bureaucrats who are not restrained from targeting high-risk groups by democratic niceties. The problem is that, given the climate of fear generated by two decades of the 'everyone-is-at-risk' nonsense, the policy now recommended by Chin and Pisani is likely to lead to more repressive interventions against stigmatised minorities (which will not help to deter the spread of HIV infection).

Chin confesses that he has found it difficult 'to understand how, over the past decade, mainstream AIDS scientists, including most infectious disease epidemiologists, have virtually all uncritically accepted the many "glorious" myths and misconceptions UNAIDS and AIDS activists continue to perpetuate'. An explanation for this shocking betrayal of principle can be found in a 1996 commentary on the British AIDS campaign entitled 'Icebergs and rocks of the "good lie"'. In this article, *Guardian* journalist Mark Lawson accepted that the public had been misled over the threat of AIDS, but argued that the end of promoting sexual restraint (especially among the young) justified the means (exaggerating the risk of HIV infection): as he put it, 'the government has lied and I am glad'.

This sort of opportunism is not confined to AIDS: in other areas where experts are broadly in sympathy with government policy—such as passive smoking, obesity and climate change—they have been similarly complicit in the prostitution of science to propaganda.

It is a pity that Chin and Pisani did not blow their whistles earlier and louder, but better late than never.

> "Africa—where some countries have
> an HIV prevalence greater than 30
> percent—offers a . . . grim example
> of what happens when we don't react
> quickly or with openness to the spread
> of HIV."

AIDS Is Devastating Africa

Stephanie Nolen

An award-winning reporter, Stephanie Nolen is the South Asia correspondent for Toronto's Globe and Mail *and author of* 28: Stories of AIDS in Africa. *In the following viewpoint, Nolen claims that the AIDS epidemic has wrought more devastation in Africa than other humanitarian crises. AIDS exacerbates the continent's existing tuberculosis and malaria epidemics, she maintains, and by lowering productivity, life expectancy, and child survival rates, AIDS robs decades of socioeconomic progress from African nations. Finally, the author concludes that the estimate of 28 million Africans living with the virus is conservative compared with her own experiences and that of doctors and health officials.*

As you read, consider the following questions:

1. Why is poverty a key factor in the AIDS crisis in Africa, according to Nolen?

2. Who is Stephen Lewis, as mentioned by the author?
3. In Nolen's opinion, what perception shapes the muted response to the AIDS epidemic in Africa?

A IDS has now been reported in every country in the world, and it is present in epidemic levels in many. Some 40 million people around the world are living with the virus. In terms of absolute numbers of people infected, India is the country with the worst epidemic, while the fastest spread of the disease is occurring in Russia and the Ukraine, among injecting drug users and prisoners. China, too, has a looming AIDS crisis, with an estimated 650,000 people infected but almost no public knowledge of the disease. But AIDS in Africa is a unique phenomenon. The epidemics in eastern Europe and Asia do not compare to what is happening in sub-Saharan Africa: the disease is spreading quickly in Russia, yes, but the prevalence, the percentage of people with HIV in the population, is barely one percent. And while India has six million people infected, the country's huge population means the prevalence is still less than one percent. Consequently, the impact, on the economy and on society, is marginal. Africa—where some countries have an HIV prevalance greater than 30 percent—offers a lesson for all of these places, a grim example of what happens when we don't react quickly or with openness to the spread of HIV.

Poverty Is Key

There is always a danger in talking about "Africa"—as if it is one place, one country, one homogeneous story. Africa is fifty-three countries, many of which are themselves made up of hundreds of peoples and cultures. Prosperous South Africa has more in common with France than it does with anarchic Somalia or the deserts of Mali. And there is no one monolithic story of AIDS in Africa. HIV infection rates range from 43 percent of pregnant women in Swaziland in the southern tip of the continent to less than one percent in Senegal on the west coast. And yet there are factors common across sub-Saharan African countries, from the legacy of colonialism to the patterns of conflict and migrant labor, which have had a direct influence on how the story of AIDS unfolded in the region.

A great many things made Africa particularly susceptible to AIDS, some of them innate to the communities where the disease flourished, and many others imposed from outside. The key one is poverty. Put simply, millions of Africans are living with a virus from which they might easily have been protected if they had had access to education about it, or to the means of defending themselves. At the same time, their lack of resources led them to do things—to sell sex, to stay with a philandering husband, to leave their families and seek work far away—that they might not otherwise have done; this too spread the disease. And the destitution and weakness of many sub-Saharan states crippled their ability to respond once their populations were infected. Congo didn't have the surveillance systems to detect or track the disease when it first emerged; Kenya didn't have the money to reach its populations with protective measures; Zambia didn't have the nurses or doctors to care for the sick; Lesotho couldn't buy the drugs that would have saved the dying.

That poverty has its roots in the colonial era, when Africa was viewed as one huge source of raw materials for the European powers, its economies deliberately undeveloped, its peoples kept, often through violent repression, as a sort of indentured workforce. Independence didn't make things much better: hard on the heels of the liberation struggles of the 1960s came the Cold War, and a different sort of meddling. The superpowers used Africa as a board in their global chess game, arming insurgencies such as Mozambique's RENAMO, propping up cooperative tyrants, assassinating elected leaders—as the CIA [US Central Intelligence Agency] did Congo's Patrice Lumumba—and warping politics and development all across the region in their ideological battle and quest for control of Africa's rich resources. In the 1980s came a new focus on development and poverty alleviation, but this was little help. The massive international financial institutions, the World Bank and the International Monetary Fund, ordered the most debt-ridden African nations to overhaul their economies or find themselves cut off from assistance. It may have looked like a good idea at the time, but structural adjustment, as it became known, was one more disaster: its ill-conceived user fees denied poor people access to whatever health and education systems existed, while its other interventions failed to produce significant economic growth. Then, in the 1990s, when more than a century of foreign meddling had reduced much of the continent to a corrupt, conflict-torn, impoverished mess, the rich donor countries in North America and Europe refused to send more money to bail out African governments, asking how they could possibly be expected to put funding into such a disaster.

On AIDS in particular, on the pandemic that emerged as an "African problem" at the height of this donor fatigue, there has been a monstrous failure to fund a response anything near commensurate with the scale of the crisis. The United Nations said the global response to AIDS needed $6.6 billion in 1999; donor nations gave $560 million. (These and all other figures are in U.S. dollars.) In 2002, the UN created the Global Fund to Fight AIDS, Tuberculosis and Malaria, intended to target the pandemic and two of its most deadly co-infections with swift and comprehensive programs. The fund struggled, from its first days, to cover its pledges to AIDS-ravaged countries; by mid-2006, it had a billion-dollar shortfall.

That said, some of the blame for the gravity of the AIDS crisis rests on the shoulders of Africans. The continent has been plagued by massive failures of leadership: by corrupt despots who plundered state coffers and exercised brutal repression on movements for democracy, and specifically by heads of state and local government who chose to shun and condemn people with AIDS rather than mobilizing resources to assist them. People in many parts of the continent still maintain cultural and social practices—such as having multiple concurrent sexual partners and eschewing condoms—in the face of the horribly obvious evidence of what AIDS is doing to their communities.

Why AIDS Is Different

When I started to write about AIDS, my editors asked a sensible question: Why single out this disease when there is so much "wrong" in Africa? Why is AIDS any different from the famines and the wars and the corruption and the dozens of other terrible diseases, the shortage of schools and clinics and clean water?

The difference is that AIDS underlies all of these things—that it is amplifying the damage even as it undermines the ability to respond. Because it targets the young, productive generation, AIDS robs countries of the people who grow the food and work in the factories and teach in the schools. It makes existing epidemics of tuberculosis and malaria a thousandfold more lethal. It makes countries more vulnerable to political instability and environmental disasters. In country after country, AIDS is stealing away the hard-won gains of the past couple of decades, lowering school enrolments, productivity levels, life expectancies, child survival rates and economic growth.

Many people at home, I know, think of AIDS as one more disaster in Africa, like the endless wars and recurring famines, as inevitable and unchanging. And yet over the last nine years . . . I have seen something change. In most of the places I travel today, people and their governments are deeply engaged in the response to AIDS, in an effort to stanch the wounds it leaves. And although the pandemic is still outstripping the response, I have seen AIDS treatment come to Africa. I was familiar with the "Lazarus effect" [where dying AIDS patients improved to almost normal] of antiretrovirals in North America, and had seen friends with AIDS become well again and flourish, but watching it happen in Africa has nevertheless been mesmerizing. I saw African activists put pressure on the pharmaceutical industry until they won access to cheap generic drugs and drove down the prices of brand-name ones. I have seen projects with limited

© Ann Telanes, 2006, Cartoonist Group

staff and minuscule budgets, working without reliable electricity or in wildly remote areas, get drugs to people in conditions—even in the middle of wars—that the West deemed impossible. I have seen people at the edge of death get suddenly, gloriously well again, just like they do at home.

Something else changed, too: the pandemic has started, very slowly, to attract political attention, media coverage and serious funding. This is due to the work of thousands of tireless African activists, and a few high-powered champions of the cause in the West—particularly Irish rock star Bono, former U.S. president Bill Clinton, software billionaire Bill Gates, and Stephen Lewis, a Canadian diplomat who from 2002 to 2007 served as the UN's Special Envoy for HIV/AIDS in Africa, a role in which he was a dogged and effective advocate for the continent's women and children. This combined pressure produced, first, the Global Fund—a unique effort to target the diseases swiftly. Then in 2003

U.S. President George W. Bush announced a five-year, $15 billion program—the President's Emergency Plan for AIDS Relief, or PEPFAR—to fund AIDS prevention and treatment in the developing world, with a focus on Africa. That program was soon mired in controversy (its architects insisted on designating funds for abstinence-based prevention efforts, and on buying brand-name drugs made by large U.S. companies instead of cheaper generic medications that could treat more people). But it was the biggest international health intervention ever attempted, and it quickly brought new attention to the African AIDS pandemic. In 2006, Bono launched the Red campaign—a marketing effort that soon had people snapping up iPods and T-shirts from The Gap in support of the Global Fund—and suddenly the crisis was trendy.

And yet the response remains muted. Few people outside Africa seem to understand the scale or the epic gravity of what is happening there. When I talk to people at home about the pandemic, I get the sense that they feel a dying African is somehow different from a dying Canadian, American or German—that Africans have lower expectations or place less value on their lives. That to be an orphaned fifteen-year-old thrust into caring for four bewildered siblings, or a teacher thrown out of her house after she tells her husband she is infected—that somehow this would be less terrifying or strange for a person in Zambia or Mozambique than it would be for someone in the United States or Britain. . . .

A Word About Numbers

Let me say, here, a word about numbers. . . . The data collection on the number of people living with HIV/AIDS in sub-Saharan Africa is extremely weak. Many countries draw their statistics only from HIV tests at prenatal clinics, because that's the one time adults reliably come into contact with the health system. But those numbers can be artificially high compared to the overall population, because by definition pregnant women have had sex. A few countries have done door-to-door surveys, and these are more reliable, but people who know or suspect they are infected are much more likely to decline to be tested by the surveyor who knocks at the door, even when promised anonymity. So that pushes the numbers in those surveys down. Many nations lack the skilled people to accurately process and maintain these kinds of statistics, and in those countries, the UN agency responsible, UNAIDS, is guessing, too. Still, today, only an estimated 10 percent of those who have the virus in Africa have actually been tested for it. Meanwhile, national governments have played down their infection rates—not wanting to scare off tourists or foreign investors—at the same time that international agencies have sometimes inflated them, out of a desire to attract more attention and more funding. In recent years UNAIDS has revised its infection numbers for most African countries downward (while a few shot up); part of that decline is the result of people dying, and part of it of more reliable statistics.

The latest epidemiological survey for the continent gives a range of twenty-five to thirty million people with the virus. My own feeling, after nine years of watching the African pandemic unfold, is that the figure twenty-eight million in Africa is conservative. Again and again, I travel to areas where the estimated prevalence is 15 percent, but it seems obvious from looking around that the rate of infection is higher; or I speak to doctors and government health officials who have just done new surveys and found much higher numbers than they expected. I suspect that when accurate survey methods finally reach into rural areas and all segments of the population, the figure will be still higher.

This is, of course, on some level immaterial. The African epidemic is as much of a crisis with twenty-eight million people infected as it is with twenty-three or thirty-three million. The inaction of the previous two decades is ample proof that numbers alone, no matter how high, are not enough to motivate the United States to respond in any adequate way to the crisis.

| "An increasing number of scientists are acknowledging that the AIDS crisis, in Africa and worldwide, is seriously distorted and overblown."

The Impact of AIDS in Africa Is Overblown

Matthew Cullinan Hoffman

Matthew Cullinan Hoffman is the Latin American correspondent for LifeSiteNews.com. In the following viewpoint, he purports that a growing number of scientists claim the AIDS epidemic is distorted and overblown, particularly in Africa. Scientists maintain that the prevalence of HIV infection varies greatly throughout the continent, which is in part due to differences in sexual behavior, Hoffman suggests. Additionally, he notes, those scientists point out the most extensive epidemics are confined to only ten sub-Saharan African nations. Organizations ignore these figures to protect the financial interests of the AIDS establishment, Hoffman contends.

As you read, consider the following questions:

1. According to James Chin, as cited by the author, how do HIV infection rates differ in South Africa, Ghana, and Senegal?

2. What does UNAIDS state in its 2006 report, as reported by Hoffman?
3. What does the author say that Edward Green alleges about condoms and HIV rates in Africa?

An increasing number of scientists are acknowledging that the AIDS crisis, in Africa and worldwide, is seriously distorted and overblown by international agencies and corporations, who in many cases tend to profit from the confusion. In recent months, more of these researchers have been speaking out against a wealthy and powerful establishment that consistently ignores fundamental facts regarding HIV and AIDS.

The controversy stems from a fundamental disagreement over almost every issue regarding AIDS transmission, prevalence, and prevention. While the United Nations Joint Program on HIV/AIDS (UNAIDS) and other international agencies insist that AIDS is a growing global epidemic that must be treated with massive condom distribution, sex education, and drug treatments, several high-profile scientists call the picture a "distortion". They say that AIDS statistics are overblown, and argue that the best means of prevention is abstinence and marital fidelity.

Dr. James Chin was the former head of a World Health Organization Global Programme on Aids unit from 1987–1992 and is currently a public health professor at [the University of California at] Berkeley. He noted in a recent interview that in reality, the AIDS "pandemic" is not as widespread as it is often portrayed, and not even in large parts of Africa, where rates of infection with the Human Immunodeficiency Virus (HIV) vary widely.

"In South Africa, close to 20 percent of the adult population is infected with HIV, whereas in Ghana, it is only 2 to 3 percent of the population, and in Senegal, less than one percent is infected," Chin told Cybercast News Service.

In a separate interview with LifeSiteNews, Chin stated that the differences between these nations and countries like South

Africa and Zimbabwe, where the rate of HIV infection is as high as 20 percent of the adult population, is at least in part due to behavioral differences, including sexual behavior. "In general, there are lower prevalence of sexual risk behaviors and HIV facilitating factors in West African populations compared to Eastern and Southern African populations," he said.

A Refusal to Acknowledge the Facts

Chin added that the United Nations Joint Program on HIV/AIDS (UNAIDS), has refused to acknowledge its own studies showing that the epidemic has stabilized or is in decline.

"Up to 2006, UNAIDS maintained its position that the pandemic was "ever-increasing and ever-expanding", noted Chin. "However in its May 2006 report to the UN, UNAIDS acknowledged that—'Overall globally, the HIV incidence rate (the annual number of new HIV infections as a proportion of previously uninfected persons) is believed to have peaked in the late 1990s and to have stabilized subsequently, notwithstanding increasing incidence in a number of countries.'"

Chin also quoted the report's admission that "changes in behavior" are at the root of the success. "In several countries, favourable trends in incidence are related to changes in behaviour and prevention programs. Changes in incidence along with rising AIDS mortality have caused global HIV prevalence (the proportion of people living with HIV) to level off," the report states.

"Since this report to the UN, I haven't seen much reference to the 'peaking' of global HIV incidence by the late 1990s—almost a decade ago—you should ask UNAIDS why they have not mentioned this more since then!" Chin told LifeSite.

Dr. James Chin has recently published a book detailing his struggles with the UNAIDS establishment. Titled "The AIDS Pandemic: The Collision of Epidemiology with Political Correctness", the book's thesis is that "the story of HIV has been distorted by UNAIDS and AIDS activists in order to support the myth of the high potential risk of HIV epidemics spreading into the general population" according to the publisher.

Chin's criticisms are echoed by two other eminent scientists at Harvard's Center on Population and Development, Dr. Edward Green and Dr. Daniel Halperin, whose research continues to be ignored by the AIDS establishment. Dr. Green has served as team leader on numerous USAID [US Agency for International Development] project designs and evaluations. Dr. Halpern is a former Technical Adviser for Prevention/Behaviour Change, USAID Southern Africa Regional HIV/AIDS Program.

A Strange Disconnect

The two Harvard scientists have noted that, while abstinence programs in countries like Uganda have proven their effectiveness, AIDS policymakers continue to promote condom use, and ignore the differences in AIDS rates among African antions.

Halperin points out that the most serious cases of high-frequency infection are confined to only 10 Sub-Saharan African nations, less than 25% of the countries of the region. "There are about 10 nations, all of them in Southern Africa, that have very bad epidemics," Halperin told Cybercast News Service. "Outside of those countries, for the most part, the rest of the world is not nearly as affected, although there are certain risk groups within some countries which have extremely high rates of HIV."

Green has written a book on Uganda's "ABC" approach to HIV transmission: first Abstinence, then Be Faithful, then if the first two fail, use a Condom. Uganda's immediate response to the AIDS threat in the early 1980s reduced the incidence of HIV infection from 15% to less than 4% in the space of a few years. Green's book examines the strange disconnect between the demonstrated effectiveness of abstinence and marital fidelity campaigns and the prevention strategies of international aid agencies.

In an article for the journal *The Responsive Community*, Green points out the utter failure of the condom-pushing approach of UNAIDS. "How has the Western risk-reduction model fared in

Africa? There is no evidence that mass promotion of condoms has paid off with a decline of HIV infection rates at the population level in Africa, according to a new UNAIDS assessment of condom effectiveness. In fact, countries with the highest levels of condom availability (Zimbabwe, Botswana, South Africa, Kenya) also have some of the highest HIV prevalence rates in the world," he writes.

Green notes that the insistence on promoting failed policies can be explained in part by a cultural bias in favor of sexual promiscuity and permissiveness, but adds that an important factor may also be the economic interests of the global AIDS establishment. "Apart from Western values and biases, there are economic factors to consider. AIDS prevention has become a billion dollar industry" he writes. "Under President Bush's global AIDS initiative, the US will spend $15 billion, partially on prevention. It would be politically naive to expect that those who profit from the lucrative AIDS-prevention industry would not be inclined to protect their interests."

"Those who work in condom promotion and STD [sexually transmitted disease] treatment, as well as the industries that supply these devices and drugs, do not want to lose market share, so to speak, to those few who have begun to talk about behavior. Put crudely, who makes a buck if Africans simply start being monogamous?"

Green's statement about organizations "protecting their interests" has proven to be prophetic. Since the initiation of the US program, which promotes abstinence as part of its approach to prevention, it has suffered continuous attacks by the global AIDS establishment, which is rigidly opposed to any serious discussion of the benefits of abstinence and marital fidelity. And despite their impeccable establishment credentials as research scientists affiliated with major universities, scientists like Green are accused of "AIDS denialism".

When Bill Gates, founder of Microsoft, merely mentioned abstinence and marital fidelity as part of the solution to the problem at an AIDS conference in Toronto last year [2006], he was roundly booed by the audience. However, when he played down such "politically incorrect" solutions and began to speak of condom distribution, he was met with enthusiastic cheering.

Despite the increasingly well-known facts about HIV transmission and prevention, certain proposals simply remain socially unacceptable among the apparatchiks [loyal bureaucrats] of the international AIDS bureaucracy. With billions of dollars of government aid money on the line, the status quo is likely to continue with saving lives kept to a low priority.

Periodical and Internet Sources Bibliography

The following articles have been selected to supplement the diverse views presented in this chapter.

William Lee Adams	"Eve of an HIV Epidemic in Romania," *Time*, September 20, 2010.
George Alleyne	"Will We Win and When?," *UN Chronicle*, June 1, 2010.
Associated Press	"Global AIDS Crisis Overblown? Some Say Yes," November 30, 2008.
Joe DeCapua	"African Gays Under Attack as HIV/AIDS Epidemic Turns 30," Voice of America News, May 13, 2011. www.voanews.com.
Don Duncan	"Growing Afghan Intravenous Heroin Use Spurs HIV Epidemic," *Deutsche Welle*, May 30, 2011.
Anthony S. Fauci	"After 30 Years of HIV/AIDS, Real Progress and Much Left to Do," *Washington Post*, May 27, 2011.
Elon Green	"The 10 Greatest Villains of the AIDS Epidemic," AlterNet, May 24, 2011. www.alternet.org.
Tamara McClintock Greenberg	"Beyond the AIDS Epidemic," *Psychology Today Blogs*, March 14, 2011. www.psychologytoday.com.
Li Xiaoshu	"The Public Face of AIDS in China," *Global Times*, February 3, 2010.
New York Times	"HIV Rises Among Young Gay Men," January 14, 2008.
Right Vision News	"USA: World AIDS Day 2010: Are We Finally Turning the Tide?," November 29, 2010.

How Can the Spread of AIDS Be Controlled?

Chapter Preface

The Centers for Disease Control and Prevention (CDC) asserts that latex condoms can prevent the transmission of HIV through sexual intercourse. "Latex condoms cover the penis and provide an effective barrier to exposure to secretions such as urethral and vaginal secretions, blocking the pathway of sexual transmission of HIV infection," it states. "Laboratory studies have demonstrated that latex condoms provide an essentially impermeable barrier to particles the size of HIV." The CDC advises that, if not used properly or consistently, they do not offer 100 percent protection. "Inconsistent use can lead to [sexually transmitted disease] acquisition because transmission can occur with a single act of intercourse with an infected partner," it explains. In this scenario, the estimated chances of HIV infection are one in five thousand with a condom and one in five hundred without.

On the other hand, critics argue that condoms have failed to cut HIV transmission rates, particularly in regions where the virus is prevalent, including Africa and Thailand. "The marketing and distribution of condoms won't solve the problem. Partner fidelity has a much better chance," contends Edward Green, the director of the Harvard AIDS Prevention Research Project. Green does support their use, albeit after monogamy and abstinence. "I am against saying that we are doing all that we can because we have exported so many cartons of condoms," he insists. Others take a harder stance, however. "Condoms are highly dangerous," proclaims Yolly Eileen Gamutan, secretary of Asia's Catholic Association of Doctors, Nurses, and Health Professionals. "Even if all brothels were required to have supplies of condoms," she continues, "and if they were available in all supermarkets, bars, restaurants, and other public gathering places, still it would not deter the widespread of HIV/AIDS." In the following chapter, the authors debate the developments and measures intended to prevent the virus from spreading.

> "Adoption of an 'opt out' approach [to routine HIV testing] could reduce public resistance to HIV testing and increase the number of people who know their HIV status."

Routine HIV Testing Could Help Control the Spread of AIDS

David McQuoid-Mason

David McQuoid-Mason is a law professor at the Centre for Socio-Legal Studies, University of KwaZulu-Natal in South Africa. In the following viewpoint, McQuoid-Mason recommends routine HIV testing during medical treatment unless the patient chooses not to, or the "opt-out" approach. Using this approach, the author states, enables more HIV-positive patients to seek treatment and prevent spreading the virus, helps survivors of sexual assault and others placed at risk for infection, and lessens the stigma surrounding AIDS. Routine HIV testing is also reasonable and justified, McQuoid-Mason suggests, because it is already practiced in democratic and open societies.

As you read, consider the following questions:

1. What conditions must be satisfied for opt-out HIV testing, according to Edwin Cameron, cited by the author?
2. Why is opt-in HIV testing a burden on health care resources, in McQuoid-Mason's opinion?
3. How has opt-in HIV testing led to discrimination, in the author's view?

Judge Edwin Cameron has suggested that because of the high level of ignorance about people's HIV status and the stigma attached to it, and as HIV infection can now be controlled through the use of antiretroviral drugs, the time has come to review the present 'opt in' approach to HIV testing and counselling. He suggests that an 'opt out' approach should be adopted whereby people receiving medical treatment should have their blood automatically tested for HIV unless they specifically opt out from doing so. He argues that this can be done provided three conditions are satisfied: (*i*) antiretroviral treatment must be made available for offer to the patient; (*ii*) there must be assurance that the consequences of diagnosis will not be discrimination and ostracism; and (*iii*) the patient must be secure in the confidentiality of the testing procedure and its outcome.

The present 'opt in' approach requires extensive counselling before HIV testing of patients and places a heavy burden on health care resources. It also inhibits people from undergoing tests because of the stigma attached to being diagnosed as HIV positive. An 'opt out' approach requires less extensive counselling and treats the test for HIV infection like that for any other sexually transmissible infection such as the routine testing of pregnant women for syphilis—unless the patient specifically refuses to be tested. Under the 'opt out' approach counselling may be done in groups or by giving patients a pamphlet or requiring them to sign a form. The high court has held that at present such conduct does not satisfy the counselling requirement for HIV testing, and that proper extensive individual counselling must be done in order to obtain an informed consent. The National Department of Health, the Health Professions Council of South Africa and the South African Medical Association have taken the same approach.

Research has shown that the adoption of an 'opt out' approach could reduce public resistance to HIV testing and increase the number of people who know their HIV status. This may lead to a rise in the uptake of people who seek access to antiretroviral treatment, as has happened in Botswana.

Judge Cameron's suggestion would mean moving away from the present 'opt in' approach and its stringent requirements for HIV testing and counselling, and regarding informed consent procedures for HIV infection like those of any other dread disease such as hepatitis B or diabetes. It has been argued that an 'opt out' approach undermines the concept of voluntariness in HIV policies, particularly in resource-poor countries where people are likely to be coerced into HIV testing by health care professionals. For this reason it is necessary to consider the likely ethical, constitutional and legal implications of such an approach in the South African context.

Ethical and Other Implications

The ethical, constitutional and legal implications of an 'opt out' approach can best be dealt with within the framework of the basic biomedical ethical principles of patient autonomy, beneficence, non-maleficence and justice.

Patient autonomy. Patient autonomy is the ethical principle that recognises that patients have the right to decide for themselves what they want to do with their bodies. The principle of autonomy is reflected in the [South African] Constitution in the rights to dignity, life, bodily integrity and privacy. The principle is also found in the National Health Act, the rules of the Health Professions Council of South Africa (HPCSA) and the common law in the provisions dealing with informed consent and confidentiality. The courts have required that informed consent for HIV testing purposes must include extensive individual pre-test counselling based on an 'opt in' approach.

An 'opt out' approach would have to ensure that patients receive sufficient information regarding the nature, effect and consequences of an HIV test to enable them to decide whether or not to consent to or assume the risk of harm involved—without subjecting them to extensive counselling as is currently required. Pamphlets, posters or group counselling may be sufficient if patients have enough information to enable them to give or refuse consent in the same manner as for any other medical test that is conducted on patients on an 'opt out' basis. In addition their right to confidentiality would have to be assured. Such an approach would be consistent with the principle of patient autonomy and the requirements of the Constitution.

Beneficence. Beneficence is the ethical principle that requires doctors and health practitioners to do good for their patients. This is reflected in the Constitution by the provision that everyone has the right of access to health care services. The principle of beneficence was apparent in the Constitutional Court judgment regarding the provision of prophylactic treatment to pregnant women and babies to prevent neonates [newborns] contracting HIV. The National Health Act also echoes the beneficence principle by requiring state-funded health departments to 'provide health services within the limits of available resources'.

The adoption of routine HIV testing would be consistent with the principle of beneficence as it would enable people who discover that they are HIV positive to seek antiretroviral treatment timeously [in a timely fashion]. It will overcome the problem of people being ignorant of their HIV status. Ignorance of their HIV status often results in HIV-positive people only seeking treatment when they have already progressed to the end stages of full-blown AIDS—by which time it may be too late. The 'opt out' approach regarding testing for HIV will also be in line with the Constitution because it will enable HIV-positive people to access health care services regarding antiretroviral drug treatment in time to save their lives—as well as to modify their sexual behaviour to save the lives of others. In order to be constitutionally acceptable—if the resources are available—access to antiretroviral treatment must be provided to patients who test HIV positive and require it.

Non-maleficence. Non-maleficence is the principle that requires doctors and health practitioners not to harm their patients. This principle is reflected in the Constitution, which provides that nobody may be refused emergency medical treatment and that everyone has a right to 'an environment that is not harmful to their health or well-being'. These provisions are also to be found in the National Health Act. An 'opt out' approach will be in line with the non-maleficence principle, particularly in respect of rape survivors and other patients at risk of being HIV positive.

Routine HIV testing of rape survivors forced to have unprotected sex is consistent with the non-maleficence principle because a negative test result gives rise to a medical emergency and the urgent need for post-exposure prophylaxis if the perpetrator may be HIV positive. Routine HIV testing of other patients will also be in accordance with the non-maleficence principle because it will ensure that those who test positive are not exposed to an environment that is harmful to their health or well-being. Once HIV-positive people know their status they can access antiretroviral treatment when they need it. They can also take steps to avoid infecting others and to prevent themselves being reinfected. In order to be consistent with the Constitution—provided the resources are available—antiretroviral treatment must be made available to patients who test HIV positive and require it.

Justice. The ethical principle of justice requires that all patients are treated equally and fairly. The Constitution provides that nobody may be unfairly discriminated against on 'one or more grounds, including race, gender, sex, pregnancy, marital status, ethnic or social origin, colour, sexual orientation, age, disability, religion, conscience, belief, culture, language and birth'. These grounds are not the only bases for discrimination, and the Constitutional Court has held that HIV status may also be a ground for discrimination. The Employment Equity Act specifically mentions HIV status as a prohibited ground of discrimination.

It can be argued that HIV-positive people are not treated equally or fairly compared with other people afflicted with deadly diseases that can be controlled through routine testing and medication. The stigma attached to HIV infection discourages people from undertaking HIV tests, and the onerous pre-test counselling requirements place an undue burden on health care providers. The result is that the majority of HIV-infected people do not know their HIV status and do not take steps to control it. In addition health care providers spend so much time pre-counselling individual patients that they can only conduct comparatively few HIV tests on a daily basis. This 'drains healthcare resources away from diagnosis and treatment of HIV'. People faced with other dread diseases are not faced with these obstacles and as they can rely on routine testing to identify their condition without being stigmatised, they can be attended to timeously by health care providers.

In a sense the current 'opt in' approach to HIV testing, with its onerous counselling procedures and the stigma associated with HIV infection, has led to HIV-positive people being unfairly discriminated against because they have been discouraged from learning their status, and as a result have been prevented from accessing life-saving treatment. An 'opt out' approach would encourage them to do so by making it easier and less stigmatising, and would be consistent with the principle of justice and fairness. The result would be that HIV-positive people would be treated like any other patients suffering from a potentially life-threatening disease who are subjected to routine testing for their own protection. As mentioned by Judge Cameron, people who test HIV positive under an 'opt out' approach should not be unfairly discriminated against or ostracised.

Routine Testing Is Reasonable

It has been argued that introducing an 'opt out' approach to HIV testing would be consistent with basic biomedical ethical principles, the Constitution and national legislation. However, if it is suggested that an 'opt out' approach is not consistent with the autonomy principles of the Constitution regarding bodily integrity and privacy, could it be argued that a law to introduce routine testing for HIV would be reasonable and justifiable? The Constitution provides that fundamental rights in the Constitution may only be limited if such limitation is of general application to the people concerned, and is reasonable and justifiable in an open and democratic society based on human dignity, equality and freedom.

A law of general application means that the law must be sufficiently clear, accessible and precise for those affected by it to know the extent of their rights and obligations. For example, if an 'opt out' approach is provided for in legislation the law would have to explain what is meant by routine testing and how people can opt out of it. The reasons for the limitation of any constitutional right must be acceptable to an open and democratic society based on human dignity, equality and freedom. It can be argued that an 'opt out' approach to HIV testing is reasonable and justifiable because it has been adopted in Botswana, and for women attending antenatal clinics in Canada, the UK and the USA. These countries are generally regarded as open and democratic societies based on human dignity, equality and freedom.

In order to satisfy the limitation requirements, the harm caused by the infringement of a constitutional right must also be proportional to the benefits to be achieved by the law. For example, any legislative interference with the autonomy rights of bodily integrity and privacy that may flow from requiring patients to 'opt out' of HIV testing would have to be less harmful than the purpose of the law. Under the 'opt out' approach the harm done to the rights of bodily integrity and privacy of patients is that patients are required to explicitly refuse an HIV test rather than request one. The purpose of the law is to enable people to discover their HIV to status without being stigmatised so that they can access treatment to save their lives and modify their sexual behaviour to save the lives of others. On balance therefore it can be strongly argued that the harm caused by shifting the onus of refusing consent is outweighed by the potentially life-saving benefits to HIV-positive patients. As a result the limitation is reasonable and justifiable in terms of the Constitution.

It is submitted that routine testing for HIV infection, using an 'opt out' approach, is consistent with the basic biomedical ethical principles of patient autonomy, beneficence, non-maleficence and justice. Such testing is also in line with the Constitution and other laws. Even if it were argued that an 'opt out' approach violated the Constitutional rights to bodily integrity and privacy such infringements would be reasonable and justifiable and therefore in accordance with the Constitution. As stated by Judge Cameron, in all instances 'the testing procedure and its outcome' must be subject to the usual rules regarding confidentiality'.

> "*[Opt-out HIV testing] clearly favors presumptive public health benefits over individual patient privacy and autonomy.*"

Routine HIV Testing Invades Privacy

Bruce Patsner

In the following viewpoint, Bruce Patsner claims that routine HIV testing based on the "opt-out" approach, or performed during medical treatment unless the patient chooses against it, infringes patient privacy. Research suggests that some individuals may alter their behavior after an HIV-positive result, but the author maintains that opt-out testing stops short of universal screening for everyone without informed consent. Moreover, he purports that the policy is at odds with state laws in which specific informed consent and pretest counseling is required for HIV testing. Patsner is an associate professor in obstetrics and gynecology at Baylor University College of Medicine.

As you read, consider the following questions:

1. What potential HIV screening strategies have been advanced by public policy officials, as described by the author?

2. For which populations has the government determined that HIV testing without consent is appropriate, as stated by Patsner?
3. What factor influences a person's likelihood to face opt-out HIV testing, in the author's opinion?

Acquired Immune Deficiency Syndrome (AIDS) remains a devastating medical illness even in the U.S. where retroviral therapy has dramatically improved the life expectancy of many individuals with the disease. AIDS is not curable but generally responds well to treatment, and some patients may have clinical remissions lasting a decade or longer. Infection with the human immunodeficiency virus (HIV) is the one essential prerequisite for an individual to develop AIDS, and all infected individuals will at some point early in the trajectory of their disease have an asymptomatic infection which can be detected by screening their blood for the presence of the HIV. Inexpensive and accurate testing methods are readily available to detect occult infection. In the U.S., approximately 25% of asymptomatic HIV-positive individuals are unaware of their seropositive status. These people can, and sometimes do, unintentionally and unknowingly transmit the disease to their sexual partners.

Without question, this situation represents a major public health crisis. Given the availability of effective treatment which can significantly diminish morbidity, and the data from some studies which suggest that at least some individuals will alter their behavior and potentially infect fewer people once they find out they are HIV-positive, there are good reasons to recommend routine screening for HIV to protect the public health. The critical questions are: Who should be screened for HIV? How aggressively should they be screened? How much informed consent, if any, should be required prior to screening?

Three potential strategies for screening for HIV for either the general population or higher-risk individuals have been advanced by public policy officials over the past ten years: (1) mandatory testing with no right of refusal; (2) voluntary testing with pretest counseling and specific informed consent (also known as "opt-in" testing); and (3) universal testing with patient notification that they will be screened for HIV unless they specifically refuse (known as "opt-out" testing). Barriers to routine screening without specific consent include concerns about low-yield and financial cost in non-high-risk populations; persistent stigma associated with HIV infection; fears that individuals who are HIV-positive will be discriminated against; laws in some states mandating counseling of individuals prior to drawing blood to screen for HIV as well as requiring a separate informed consent in order to screen; reluctance on the part of the medical profession to perform diagnostic testing on patients without informing them of what they are being tested for; and case law favoring privacy concerns as well as disciplinary actions against physicians for non-consented HIV testing on competent patients.

How Much Consent Should Be Required?

The federal government already has determined that screening without consent is appropriate for certain populations. These include prospective recruits for U.S. armed services and inmates in federal penitentiaries. These federal screening policies have survived challenge in court. The U.S. also prohibits the admission of any alien into the U.S. if they are known to be HIV-positive, though there is no requirement that aliens seeking to enter the US be screened without their consent. Within the medical profession controversy still exists about mandatory or routine screening for pregnant women despite the potential to dramatically reduce the chance of HIV transmission from an infected woman to her child while still in utero [unborn]. Some bio-ethicists have also suggested that HIV testing without consent be carried out in critically ill patients unable to consent to testing.

The CDC (Centers for Disease Control and Prevention) in Atlanta has been issuing guidelines for routine HIV testing and

The Downside of Routine Testing

Medical professional organizations, including the American Medical Association, have decried mandatory HIV testing as a threat to patient autonomy and to the patient-doctor relationship. Mandatory testing has the potential to lead to an informalization of the consent and notification process, which increases the likelihood that a patient may be tested without his or her knowledge, thus undermining the public's trust of physicians. Professional organizations have also expressed concerns that mandatory HIV testing may discourage some pregnant women from seeking medical care.

Daniel Zank, Virtual Mentor,
September 2007.
http://virtualmentor.ama-assn.org.

counseling for years, and up until 2005 had recommended "opt-in" routine testing for HIV in areas and patient populations of higher prevalence, such as individuals with other sexually transmitted diseases, known intravenous drug users, or homosexual or bisexual men. The recommendations changed, however, in 2006.

New Proposals

In 2006 the CDC published newer recommendations for HIV screening testing which advocated for "opt-out" testing. This change in policy clearly favors presumptive public health benefits over individual patient privacy and autonomy.

The new "opt-out" strategy—though a change from the previous purely voluntary and specific consented screening recommendation even for highest risk individuals—stops short of non-consented universal testing for all individuals in every potential medical care setting. The new CDC proposal acknowledges two fundamental truths about screening for occult HIV infection: (1) testing below a certain level of probability of finding a previously unknown positive result cannot be justified on economic grounds; and (2) some attention must be paid to informing patients that they will be tested.

The new CDC recommendation is to screen all patients aged 13 to 64, at the time of any hospital admission and at the time they present for out-patient care in a clinical setting where the expectation is that at least 1 per 1000 patients (0.1%) will screen positive for HIV. This new screening strategy would be for everyone in the target age range, regardless of their risk of being HIV-positive.

Many, but not all, medical organizations have come out in support of this new screening recommendation. Since neither the survival rate nor general treatment approach for AIDS has changed in the past three years [2008–2005], and no new evidence has emerged that patients are altering potentially risky behavior, it is unclear why the CDC changed its policy on testing. Adding to the confusion is that new policy is at odds with laws in many states which require specific informed consent to screen for HIV and for patients to undergo AIDS counseling prior to being screened for HIV.

Can New Guidelines Be Justified?

Although the exact reasoning used by the CDC is unclear, the new CDC recommendations may be the result of several factors, the cumulative effect of which has spurred CDC to take a more aggressive position on AIDS testing. First, AIDS and HIV infection from unknowing partners continues to be a problem despite voluntary programs. This is clearly a frustrating situation for public health officials. There has been no significant improvement in the new infection rate in the U.S. between the 2004 and 2006 recommendations, and perhaps the new recommendations belie a belief that population screening goals will not be met without further change in screening policy.

Additionally, there is now more support from medical organizations in favor of mandatory testing of patients who present for any type of medical care. There is also a general recognition that private, home testing availability has not resulted in a lowering of the incidence of new cases—if they are used at all—and an acknowledgment that fear of the results might prevent an individual from self-testing despite the possible risk to the public health. Lastly, it appears that the purely voluntary testing system is not working.

All of these CDC concerns may be completely legitimate from a medical point of view, but they provide no substantive basis as to why public health concerns should trump the recognized patient privacy and specific informed consent issues.

Medical and Legal Challenges

The recommendations/guidelines from the CDC carry some weight with public health policy experts but do not have the force of law. The United States Supreme Court has not yet faced the issue of whether it is constitutional to screen for HIV without obtaining an individual's specific informed consent or counseling on AIDS. Until 2005, specific consent for HIV testing was required in all fifty-three U.S. states and territories, but the situation is now one characterized by a lack of uniformity of state laws. At present, the most that can be said is that an individual's likelihood of facing opt-out screening for HIV at a medical clinic or at the time of admission to the hospital depends on which state he or she is in at the time.

The primary argument for routine, non-consented HIV screening is that it offers individuals the opportunity to become aware of their HIV status and change their behavior so that infection of others might be prevented. Public health experience and patient behavior with other venereal diseases (e.g., syphilis, herpes, human papillomavirus infection) calls this basic assumption into question; this is one reason why some medical societies do not support "opt-out" screening of hospitalized patients. Even if behavioral data definitively supported a switch from "opt-in" to "opt-out" testing, it still begs the question of whether this public health concern should now trump traditional legal protections of patient privacy and due process rights. Apparently some states, the CDC, and many medical societies now think it should. Whether federal courts will answer this question the same way remains to be seen.

> "[The pope] said that . . . in some cases,
> such as for male prostitutes, [condom]
> use could represent a first step in
> assuming moral responsibility."

The Catholic Church May Allow Condom Use in Some Cases

Associated Press

In the following viewpoint, the Associated Press (AP) suggests that the Catholic Church accepts condom use to reduce the spread of AIDS in certain situations. In a recent book, Pope Benedict XVI declared that male prostitutes begin to show moral responsibility when they use condoms to protect themselves or others from HIV infection, AP states. The pope's comments are a stunning departure from his controversial statement that condoms exacerbate the AIDS crisis and the Catholic Church's long opposition to artificial contraception, AP explains. Headquartered in New York City, AP is one of the largest news-gathering networks in the world.

As you read, consider the following questions:

1. What does Pope Benedict XVI state about condoms as a solution, as quoted by the author?

2. Who is the Vatican's top official on bioethics and sexuality, according to the Associated Press?

3. In what instance in the 1960s did the Vatican view contraception as a lesser of two evils, as claimed by the author?

Pope Benedict XVI has opened the door on the previously taboo subject of condoms as a way to fight HIV, saying male prostitutes who use condoms may be beginning to act responsibly. It's a stunning comment for a pontiff who has blamed condoms for making the AIDS crisis worse.

The pope made the comments in an interview with a German journalist published as a book entitled "Light of the World: The Pope, the Church and the Signs of the Times," which is being released Tuesday. The Vatican newspaper *L'Osservatore Romano* ran excerpts on Saturday.

Church teaching has long opposed condoms because they are a form of artificial contraception, although the Vatican has never released an explicit policy about condoms and HIV. The Vatican has been harshly criticized for its position.

Benedict said that condoms are not a moral solution to stopping AIDS. But he said in some cases, such as for male prostitutes, their use could represent a first step in assuming moral responsibility "in the intention of reducing the risk of infection."

Benedict made the comment in response to a general question about Africa, where heterosexual HIV spread is rampant.

He used as a specific example male prostitutes, for whom contraception is not usually an issue, but did not mention married couples where one spouse is infected. The Vatican has come under pressure from even church officials to condone condom use for such monogamous married couples to protect the uninfected spouse from transmission.

Benedict drew the wrath of the United Nations, European governments and AIDS activists when, en route to Africa in 2009, he told reporters that the AIDS problem on the continent couldn't be resolved by distributing condoms. "On the contrary, it increases the problem," he said then.

Journalist Peter Seewald, who interviewed Benedict over the course of six days this summer, raised the Africa condom comments, asking him if it wasn't "madness" for the Vatican to forbid a high-risk population from using condoms.

"There may be a basis in the case of some individuals, as perhaps when a male prostitute uses a condom, where this can be a first step in the direction of a moralization, a first assumption of responsibility," Benedict said.

Asked if that meant that the church wasn't opposed in principle to condoms, the pope replied:

The church "of course does not regard it as a real or moral solution, but in this or that case, there can be nonetheless in the intention of reducing the risk of infection, a first step in a movement toward a different way, a more human way, of living sexuality."

Elsewhere in the book he reaffirmed church teaching opposing artificial contraception.

"How many children are killed who might one day have been geniuses, who could have given humanity something new, who could have given us a new Mozart or some new technical discovery?" he asked rhetorically.

He reiterated the church's position that abstinence and marital fidelity is the only sure way to prevent HIV.

The English publisher of the book, Rev. Joseph Fessio, said the pope was not justifying condom use as a lesser of two evils.

"This is not a justification," he said. Rather, "The intention of protecting the other from disease, of using a condom, may be a sign of an awakening moral responsibility."

However, the Rev. Jim Martin, a Catholic writer, said the comments were certainly a departure, an exception where there had never been an exception before.

"While some bishops and archbishops have spoken in this way, the pope has never affirmed this," Martin said. "And it's interesting that he uses as an example someone who is trying to act morally to someone else by not passing on an infection, which was always the stance of those people who favored condoms in cases of HIV and AIDS. So it does mark a departure."

The English translation of the original German specified "male prostitute." The Italian translation in *L'Osservatore Romano*, however, used the feminine "prostitute." The discrepancy wasn't immediately clear.

Cardinal Elio Sgreccia, the Vatican's longtime top official on bioethics and sexuality, elaborated on the pontiff's comments, stressing that it was imperative to "make certain that this is the only way to save a life." Sgreccia told the Italian news agency ANSA that that is why the pope on the condom issue "dealt with it in the realm of the exceptional."

The condom question was one that "needed an answer for a long time," Sgreccia said. "If Benedict XVI raised the question of exceptions, this exception must be accepted . . . and it must be verified that this is the only way to save life. This must be demonstrated," Sgreccia said.

In the 1960s, the Vatican itself condoned giving contraceptive pills to nuns at risk of rape by fighters in the Congo to prevent pregnancy, arguing that the contraception was a lesser evil than pregnancy.

Archbishop Gregory Aymond of New Orleans said clearly the pope wasn't encouraging condom use.

"I think the pope has been very strong in saying condoms do not solve the problem of morality and do not solve the problem of good sex education. But if a person chooses not to follow the teaching of Christ in the church, they are at least obliged to prevent another person from contracting a disease that is deadly," he said.

In Africa, Benedict's comments drew praise among gays and AIDS activists.

"If he's talking about condoms, it's a step in the right direction," said David Kamau, who heads the nonprofit Kenya

Treatment Access Movement. "It's accepting the reality on the ground. . . . If the Church has failed to get people to follow its moral values and practice abstinence, they should take the next best step and encourage condom use."

John Kitte, a gay Ugandan, said the pope was acting as a good parent.

"He minds about all the people living on earth. What he has suggested is very good and I encourage gays to take his advice seriously."

But an evangelist pastor in the Uganda capital of Kampala, Solomon Male, argued the pope shouldn't be granting any recognition of or encouragement to gays.

"If the Pope is saying so, then he has not read the Bible," he said. "Gay acts are bad. It is abominable and should not take place."

Christian Weisner, of the pro-reform group We Are Church in the pope's native Germany, said the pope's comments were "surprising, and if that's the case one can be happy about the pope's ability to learn."

| "*[It] doesn't mean in any sense that [the pope is] saying the use of condoms is a good thing.*"

The Catholic Church Does Not Endorse Condom Use

Raymond Burke, as told to John Burger

Raymond Burke is an American cardinal of the Catholic Church and the prefect of the Supreme Tribunal of the Apostolic Signatura (the court of final appeal) at the Vatican. John Burger is news editor of the National Catholic Register, *an American newspaper. In the following viewpoint, Burke insists that the Catholic Church does not endorse condoms as a moral or viable solution to the AIDS epidemic. Pope Benedict XVI clearly stated that condom use, in the case of male prostitutes, is a step toward understanding that such activity is immoral and trivializes sex, Burke maintains. It was the media that misinterpreted the pope's statements as a compromise on condoms, Burke asserts, while the church's teaching on sexuality has not changed.*

As you read, consider the following questions:

1. What examples does Burger provide of the media's making assumptions that the pope is open to condoms in

Raymond Burke and John Burger, "What the Pope Really Meant," *National Catholic Register*, November 29, 2010. Copyright © 2010 by National Catholic Register. All rights reserved. Reproduced by permission.

some cases?

2. According to Burger, what statement did the Vatican Press Office issue following the pope's statement on condoms?

3. What does the pope claim about the "fixation" on condoms, as quoted in the viewpoint?

Cardinal Raymond Burke is prefect of the Supreme Tribunal of the Apostolic Signatura, the court of final appeal at the Vatican.

The Wisconsin native is the first American to hold that curial [church governmental] position. Pope Benedict XVI, who appointed him to the post in 2008, elevated him to cardinal Nov. 20, [2010,] along with another American, Cardinal Donald Wuerl of Washington, D.C., and 22 other bishops and archbishops from around the world.

In the midst of activities related to the consistory of Nov. 22 [a gathering of the cardinals], Cardinal Burke took some time to read an advance copy of *Light of the World: The Pope, the Church, and the Signs of the Times*, Pope Benedict's book-length interview with German journalist Peter Seewald, just as a controversy about the Pope's views on condom use broke in the press. Cardinal Burke discussed the issue by phone Nov. 24 with *Register* news editor John Burger.

[John Burger:] In Light of the World, *Peter Seewald poses the objection that "it is madness to forbid a high-risk population (AIDS) to use condoms. To which Pope Benedict answers, in part, "There may be a basis in the case of some individuals, as perhaps when a male prostitute uses a condom, where this can be a first step in the direction of a moralization, a first assumption of responsibility, on the way toward recovering an awareness that not everything is allowed and that one cannot do whatever one wants. But it is not really the way to deal with the evil of HIV infection. That can really lie only in a humanization of sexuality."*

Seewald asks for a clarification: "Are you saying, then, that the Catholic Church is actually not opposed in principle to the use of condoms?" The Pope answers, "She of course does not regard it as a real or moral solution, but in this or that case, there can be, nonetheless, in the intention of reducing the risk of infection, a first step in a movement toward a different way, a more human way, of living sexuality."

What is the Pope saying here? Is he saying that in some cases condoms can be permitted?

[Raymond Cardinal Burke:] No, he is not. I don't see any change in the Church's teaching. What he's commenting on—in fact, he makes the statement very clearly that the Church does not regard the use of condoms as a real or a moral solution—in the point he makes about the male prostitute is a certain conversion process taking place in an individual's life. He's simply making the comment that if a person who is given to prostitution at least considers using a condom to prevent giving the disease to another person—even though the effectiveness of this is very questionable—this could be a sign of someone who is having a certain moral awakening. But in no way does it mean that prostitution is morally acceptable, nor does it mean that the use of condoms is morally acceptable. The point the Pope is making is about a certain growth in freedom, an overcoming of an enslavement to a sexual activity that is morally wrong so that this concern to use a condom in order not to infect a sexual partner could at least be a sign of some moral awakening in the individual, which one hopes would lead the individual to understand that his activity is a trivialization of human sexuality and needs to be changed.

Not Compromising on Condoms

Is "the world" assuming too quickly that the Pope all of a sudden is open to "compromising" on condoms, that this may be a small yet significant opening toward "enlightenment" for the Catholic

Church? For example: "In rare cases, Pope justifies use of condoms" (New York Times). *"Condoms OK" in some cases—Pope* (BBC). Boston Herald: *quoting male prostitutes saying "too little too late, but it may encourage condom use, and that's a good thing."*

From what I've seen of the coverage in the media, I think that's correct, that that's what they're trying to suggest. But if you read the text, there's no suggestion of that at all. It's clear that the Pope is holding to what the Church has always taught in these matters. He starts out—the context of the question—by saying that when he was asked this question on the plane on his way to his pastoral visit to Africa, he felt that he was being provoked, and he wanted to draw attention to all that the Church is doing to care for AIDS victims. In Africa, the Church is the main agent of care for the AIDS victims, and so he was trying to draw some attention to that.

The text itself makes it very clear that the Church does not regard it as a real or moral solution. And when he says that it could be a first step in a movement toward a different, more human way of living sexuality, that doesn't mean in any sense that he's saying the use of condoms is a good thing.

If the media has misunderstood it, is this perhaps a failure of Pope Benedict XVI and the Vatican to communicate effectively? Is there a need to "dumb things down" so the media gets it?

I believe the fact that the media has interpreted this in a way, at least from what I can gather from the communications that I've received, that is false and is rather widespread, that it will be rather important for the Holy See now to clarify the matter. [The Vatican Press Office did indeed issue a clarification Nov. 22, saying, "The Pope again makes it clear that his intention was not to take up a position on the problem of condoms in general; his aim, rather, was to forcefully reaffirm that the problem of AIDS cannot be solved simply by distributing condoms, because much more needs to be done: prevention, education, help, advice, accompaniment, both to prevent people from falling ill and to help them if they do.]

That's what's going to have to happen now, because even some of the commentators who might be in general well disposed to the Holy See could misinterpret this and take it that indeed the Holy Father is making some change in the Church's position in regards to the use of condoms, and that would be very sad.

Did you see any Catholic commentary on this, e.g., Janet Smith, who holds the Father Michael J. McGivney Chair of Life Ethics at Sacred Heart Major Seminary in Detroit? Do you agree with her interpretation?

I did. I thought it was a good commentary. It's quite accurate. She goes into it quite in depth. She might have underlined a little bit more the words of the Holy Father himself, although she does: When she was asked if the Pope is indicating whether heterosexuals who have HIV could reduce the wrongness of their acts by condoms, she says, "No, in his second answer, he says the Church does not find condoms to be a real or a moral solution." Again, she repeats, "the intention to reduce the transmission of an infection is a first step in a movement toward a different way, a more human way, of living sexuality." That is, the *intention* is the first step, but that doesn't mean that the Holy Father is justifying the *means* by which the person wants to fulfill that intention.

Reviewing the Conversation on Sexuality

So, if nothing has changed in Catholic teaching on sexuality or the use of condoms, has this conversation changed anything?

I don't see it at all. What I see is the Holy Father is presenting a classical position of the Church from her moral theology. Self-mastery, self-discipline is not an immediate accomplishment, so we have to understand that it may take people time to reform their lives. But that doesn't suggest that he's diminishing the moral analysis of the immoral actions of the male prostitute, for instance.

It seems that perhaps some of what he says in the answers to Seewald's questions might lead to a renewed conversation on the nature of married love and sexuality.

That's what I would hope, and I think that's what the Holy Father was suggesting in the beginning of that part of the conversation with Peter Seewald, where he engages in that whole point about the trivialization of human sexuality. He says, for instance: The fact of the matter is people have access to condoms. That shows us in fact, as he points out, that condoms don't resolve the question, and that's when he begins, "the sheer fixation on the condom implies a sort of banalization of sexuality, which after all is precisely the dangerous source of the attitude of no longer seeing sexuality as an expression of love, but only a certain sort of drug that people administer to themselves." He talks about the whole fight against the banalization and dehumanization of sexuality and the need to see human sexuality as a positive good. And sexual activity as having a positive effect on the whole of man's being, being an expression of man's goodness. So that's the context, and I would hope that this matter, going forward, being clarified, will offer the real possibility of teaching more clearly about human sexuality.

Periodical and Internet Sources Bibliography

The following articles have been selected to supplement the diverse views presented in this chapter.

Mike Adams	"HIV Vaccines Cause 50 Percent False Positive Rate in HIV Tests," *InfoWars.com*, July 20, 2010. www.infowars.com.
Scott Baldaulf	"On World AIDS Day, Infection Rates Are Declining, but Dwindling Funds Threaten Progress," *Christian Science Monitor*, November 30, 2010.
Sigrid Fry-Revere	"Making HIV Tests Routine Threatens Patients' Privacy," *Chicago Sun-Times*, June 9, 2007.
Pius Kamau	"Islam, Condoms, and AIDS," *Huffington Post*, August 24, 2008.
Frances Kissling	"Condoms and Common Sense," *Religion Dispatches*, November 29, 2010.
Sanford F. Kuvin	"Our Country Is Failing the AIDS Test," *Washington Post*, November 30, 2008.
Guatam Naik	"Vaccine Shows Promise in Preventing HIV Infection," *Wall Street Journal*, September 25, 2009.
Jonathan Stern	"Better the Devil You Know? Disappointed and Disillusioned with the President's HIV & AIDS Agenda," *Conscience*, Spring 2011.
Rebecca Trager	"Success at Last for Anti-HIV Gel," *Nature News*, July 20, 2010.
Daniel Zank	"Is It Time to Revisit Prenatal HIV Testing Laws?," *Virtual Mentor*, September 2007.

OPPOSING
VIEWPOINTS®
SERIES

How Should AIDS Be Treated?

Chapter Preface

Nevirapine is an antiretroviral drug used to suppress the viral load—the amount of active HIV in an infected person's blood—and slow the progression of AIDS. It was approved by the US Food and Drug Administration (FDA) for adults in 1996 and for children in 1998. Also sold under the trade name Viramume, nevirapine is used to treat HIV-1—the predominant subtype of the virus—and prevent its transmission from mother to child during pregnancy as well as during labor and breast-feeding. In June 2011, it was announced that a rollout of antiretrovirals, including nevirapine, spared sixty-seven thousand newborns in South Africa from contracting HIV. "It is winnable to prevent all HIV-positive mothers from passing the virus on to their babies, but we now have to concentrate on the care of babies after birth," says Precious Robinson, deputy director of the South African government's prevention of mother-to-child HIV infection program.

However, others allege that nevirapine is a dangerous drug with life-threatening side effects. An investigative journalist who protests HIV as the cause of AIDS, Celia Farber argues that the FDA and other regulatory agencies have warned of the antiretroviral's toxic effects, particularly to the liver. "It seemed to me that the drug's toxicity was different from other AIDS drugs I'd studied over the years," she states. Also, Farber brings up the case of a man on nevirapine who was hospitalized after developing Stevens-Johnson Syndrome, a rare and severe disorder in which the skin dies and falls off. "Having been on life support, his organs failing, and finally left blind, without even tear ducts to enable him to cry. And still, in his mind," she exclaims, "it was HIV that was the greatest threat to his survival." In the following chapter, the authors present their views on the effectiveness of HIV/AIDS therapies.

> "The typical HIV-infected person now receiving potent combination ART lives at least 13–14 years longer than if he or she were to forgo this therapy."

AIDS Drug Treatments Prolong Lives

Sten H. Vermund

Sten H. Vermund is director of the Institute of Global Health and professor of pediatrics at Vanderbilt University School of Medicine. In the following viewpoint, Vermund asserts that antiretroviral therapy is effective in the treatment of HIV. Combination antiretroviral therapy prolongs an HIV patient's life by at least thirteen to fourteen years beyond that of a patient who forgoes the therapy—saving approximately three million years of life in the entire population—he claims. In addition, Vermund states, the use of antiretroviral therapy has successfully blocked the transmission of the virus from mother to infant. Nonetheless, he contends that barriers to HIV testing, care, and prevention persist.

As you read, consider the following questions:

1. What roles do HIV-positive people play in the implemen-

Adapted from Sten H. Vermund, "Millions of Life-Years Saved with Potent Antiretroviral Drugs in the United States: A Celebration, with Challenges," *Journal of Infectious Diseases*, 2006, vol. 194, pp. 81–85. Copyright © 2006 by Oxford University Press. All rights reserved. Reproduced by permission.

tation of antiretroviral therapy, in Vermund's view?

2. How do HIV drugs save money, according to the author?
3. What is the first "barrier to care," as described by Vermund?

[A]IDS researchers Rochelle] Walensky et al. estimate the benefits that have been gained from multidrug antiretroviral therapies (ARTs) since 1989. Their finding of ~3 million years of life saved in the United States quantifies ART benefits at the population level, complementing the well-known data on plummeting US death rates and lower AIDS case report rates noted in the era of potent therapy. The authors' detailed sensitivity analyses, varying key estimated parameters in their models, indicate that less-conservative assumptions generate an estimate of >5 million years of life saved, a plausible "higher-end" estimate of benefit. The typical HIV-infected person now receiving potent combination ART lives at least 13–14 years longer than if he or she were to forego this therapy or if it were otherwise unavailable. Quantifying the survival benefits of expanded diagnosis and modern care suggests that the economic and humanitarian benefits are greater than were hitherto appreciated.

Developing drugs, testing them without undue delay, accelerating their regulatory approval, and making them widely available have saved lives. That an average of ~200,000 persons in the United States have lived an additional year in each of the past 15 years suggests the gift given to those in need from the labor of many. Drugs are discovered and developed by biochemists, pharmaceutical developers, animal modelers, formulation chemists, microbiologists, pharmacologists, and many others in the pharmaceutical industry, in academia, at research institutes, and in government. Drugs are tested for safety and efficacy by clinical-trials experts, research-study nurses, clinical-trials volunteers, community activists, government scientists and science managers, community workers, health-care providers, pharmacists, ethical-review staff, and allied health workers. After drug approval through the work of pharmaceutical companies and regulatory-oversight experts, implementation depends on health-care workers, blood bankers, social workers, mental-health professionals, substance-abuse treatment providers, journalists, science writers, medical editors, spiritual leaders, corporate and small business leaders, enlightened insurers, and family and friends of patients challenged to receive lifelong polypharmacy. (Of course, our public-health workers in health education and promotion, epidemiology, and community prevention efforts are credited, together with community prevention activists, for laboring to reduce the need for these drugs altogether.) Political and policy leaders influence research and care investments even as health activists push the system to be more responsive and efficient. Central to implementation are the HIV-infected persons themselves, who, by the tens of thousands, keep their appointments, take pills, eliminate or reduce high-risk behaviors, and support peers who struggle with the promising but complex world of daily, lifelong therapy. The model of Walensky et al. gives all of us, from our complementary disciplines, cause for celebration.

The First Antiretroviral Agent

Zidovudine was the first approved antiretroviral agent, offering benefits that were exciting but, ultimately, only transient, because of the HIV drug resistance resulting from monotherapy. Walensky et al. have assumed a small contribution from *Pneumocystis jiroveci* prophylaxis [prevention] but no net benefit from zidovudine monotherapy alone, presumably on the basis of the results of the European Concorde study. Their latter assumption is debatable. Inclusion of survival benefits from zidovudine monotherapy would increase the lives-saved calculus—another conservative bias, in any case. Dual therapy proved to be much superior to monotherapy, and triple therapy was a huge advance, in turn, over the use of 2 drugs. This research progress and its health impact, as documented by Walensky et al., can be seen as a continuum dating from the discovery of the syndrome in 1981 and of the virus in 1983 through the successive approval of each of the 4 drug classes since 1987. This latter-20th-century advance in antiviral therapy has its centennial parallel in the golden era of microbiology and vaccine and drug development in the late 19th and early 20th centuries. Of course, [virology pioneers Louis] Pasteur, [Robert] Koch, and their peers were empiricists with little grasp of the microbiology known today; 21st century grounding in molecular methods augurs well for future discoveries leading to an eventual cure for HIV infection, flushing out and killing virus that is latent in deep tissues. This may be a good time for our national political leaders to reconsider their decision to slow the growth of the budget of the US National Institutes of Health, now lagging behind the rate of inflation.

Use of ART to block HIV transmission from mother to infant has virtually eliminated pediatric HIV infection as a major public-health problem in the United States and other economically prosperous nations. Easier-to-implement nevirapine and nevirapine-zidovudine regimens were developed that could be applied anywhere in the world, as with the "Call to Action" program (sponsored by the Elizabeth Glaser Pediatric AIDS Foundation and the Bill and Melinda Gates Foundation) and the Thai government initiative. Drugs suitable for treating pediatric-age patients with HIV infection are readily available in the United States but are less so in resource-limited nations.

In the late 1990s, activists cajoled the pharmaceutical industry into lower drug prices. Combined with lower drug prices due to competition from producers of generic drugs (including in the United States), a major effort to provide ART to infected persons in developing countries began through multinational, bilateral, and national initiatives. These are lowering HIV mortality rates in resource-limited settings, just as they did earlier in the economically richer nations. A lethal disease has been transformed into a chronic, manageable condition wherever health services delivery, financing, drug logistics (especially critical in rural areas and developing countries), health manpower, health policy, and health psychology are applied successfully.

The Importance of Detection

Walensky et al. highlight the importance of detecting all persons infected and providing care to all those who know their HIV status. Innovation is needed on many fronts. The state of North Carolina identifies acutely infected, hyperinfectious persons, to provide them with risk-reduction counseling even before antibodies are detectable. Brief health education messages that are designed for clinicians to deliver within the care setting have assisted persons in HIV care to reduce their high-risk behaviors. Practitioners in lower-prevalence regions suggest minimizing pretest counseling through interview-based risk triage, reserving their staff time for the essential posttest counseling sessions. Rapid tests are used widely in developing-world settings to cut costs and avoid the loss to follow-up inherent in an ELISA [enzyme-linked immunosorbent assay] screening (a result of the inability to provide a same-day result with an ELISA). Rapid tests are an innovation used far less often in the United States than they should be. Antenatal care programs should offer "opt-out" testing—that is, HIV testing that is routine in pregnant women, excluding only those women actively requesting to forgo the test. Efforts to increase voluntary counseling and testing and knowledge of HIV status include couples counseling to reduce marital strife and to maximize family-centered care and prevention. These are but a few examples of innovations in the diagnosis, care, and prevention of HIV infection.

Saving Lives, Saving Money

Drugs that save lives are likely to save society money, because it is cheaper to care for persons with drugs in an outpatient setting than to care for them in intensive care units, acute-care hospital beds, long-term care facilities, and hospices. Restoring economic productivity and parent-based child care saves so-called indirect costs, and fewer emergency-department visits and hospital stays save direct costs to the health-care system. Further investment in outpatient care should emphasize voluntary counseling and testing programs for HIV diagnosis that are integrated into routine medical care. This must include bridges to care for those infected. The humanitarian benefits are self-evident but may not drive investment as strongly as economic arguments can. Savings may accrue to one provider (e.g., reduced unreimbursed inpatient care expenses to a hospital or lower third-party payments), but costs may be incurred by another source (e.g., Ryan White Care Act funds). Hence, policy makers may see only their costs without knowledge of direct benefits or the savings in a different bailiwick. Early indications are that savings from outpatient management substantially outweigh the costs of the ART-based outpatient treatment programs, both here in the United States and abroad, but good data are scarce.

Barriers to Care

The millions of life-years saved in the United States should reinvigorate policy debates as to how best to identify HIV-infected persons in our country by offering and encouraging testing as a routine part of medical screening. We must reduce barriers to care, the first of which is the difficulty with which a test is obtained in many venues. We do not require extensive, expensive, time-consuming, and intimidating pretest counseling before screening for diabetes, for example, another disease that is lethal if unmanaged but that is controllable with lifelong medication. Yet many US guidelines demand substantial counseling infrastructures that may discourage primary-care providers from offering HIV tests as easily as they can offer a urine dipstick for glucose to screen for diabetes. Posttest counseling is essential for psychosocial assistance, a bridge to HIV-related health care, and needed to reduce high-risk behaviors, but pretest counseling can be made more efficient to reduce at least one barrier of time and money.

We now face a daunting challenge to do better. From 3 to 5 million person-years of life have been saved for persons living in the United States from 1989 to 2003, but do we know enough about the barriers to prompt diagnosis and effective referral to care? Are we doing enough about those barriers that we do recognize? If we address systematically the barriers to testing, care, and prevention, then future modelers will describe the *next* 15-year period as having saved *hundreds* of millions of life-years, not just in North America but around the globe.

| "[Antiretroviral treatment] does not
  prolong life."

AIDS Drug Treatments Do Not Prolong Lives

Henry Bauer

Henry Bauer is professor emeritus of chemistry and science studies and dean emeritus of arts and sciences at Virginia Tech and author of The Origin, Persistence, and Failings of HIV/AIDS Theory. *In the following viewpoint, he asserts that antiretroviral drugs do not extend life. Bauer links fewer AIDS deaths to the diagnostic redefinitions of the disease and the phasing out of highly toxic antiretroviral drugs. He argues that the median age of death for AIDS patients—around 40 years old—has not changed since the start of the AIDS era. In fact, Bauer alleges that HIV is not a causative agent of death and is no more than an indicator of a physiological problem.*

As you read, consider the following questions:

1. How did the diagnosis of AIDS change in 1993, as stated by Bauer?
2. How does Bauer compare testing HIV-positive to a fever?

3. How many HIV/AIDS deaths during the period 1987 to 1996 does the author attribute to the toxicity of AZT?

D<small>*eath rates are down, yet AIDS patients are not living longer!*</small> *Why not?*

In the early 1980s, a diagnosis of "AIDS" typically had been followed by death within a year or two. At that time, diagnosis was on the basis of Kaposi's sarcoma or of manifest opportunistic fungal infections—Pneumocystis carinii pneumonia or candidiasis.

Following the adoption of "HIV-positive" as a necessary criterion for an AIDS diagnosis, an increasing range of non-opportunistic infections and other illnesses came to be included as "AIDS-defining" (for instance, tuberculosis, wasting, cervical cancer, etc.); the most consequential changes were in 1987 and in 1993. The only basis for them was that people with some illnesses were quite often "HIV-positive", in other words, there were correlations with "HIV-positive" status, not any proof that "HIV encephalopathy", "HIV wasting disease", or other additions to the list of "AIDS-defining" conditions were caused by "HIV". Indeed, there could not be such proof since mechanisms by which "HIV" could cause illness have not been demonstrated, and they remain to this day a matter for speculation—even over the central issue of how HIV (supposedly) kills immune-system cells. An absurd consequence of these re-definitions, often cited by HIV/AIDS skeptics, is that a person suffering indisputably from tuberculosis (say) might or might not be classed as an HIV/AIDS patient, depending solely on "HIV" tests.

As "AIDS" was being diagnosed increasingly among people less desperately ill than the original AIDS victims, survival time after diagnosis became longer.

The 1993 change extended the umbrella of "AIDS patient" to cover people with no manifest symptoms of ill health; in ordinary parlance, they weren't ill, and consequently the interval between an AIDS diagnosis and death was bound to increase

153

dramatically. This re-definition also expanded enormously the number of "AIDS cases": about 70% of them are not ill.

In 1996, earlier treatment for AIDS with high-dose reverse transcriptase inhibitors like AZT [azidothymidine] (ZDV [zidovudine], Retrovir) was increasingly superseded by "highly active antiretroviral treatment" (HAART), which has been generally credited with the prolonging of lives by a considerable number of years. According to the Antiretroviral Therapy Collaboration, life expectancy for 20-year-old HIV-positives had increased by 13 years between 1996 and 2005 to an additional 49 years; for 35-year-olds, the life expectancy in 1996–99 was said to be another 25 years. According to [researcher Rochelle] Walensky et al., survival after an AIDS diagnosis now averages more than 14 years. . . .

There is general agreement, then, that antiretroviral treatment has yielded substantial extension of life to people already diagnosed with AIDS. The interval between an AIDS diagnosis and death should now be measured in decades rather than a year or two.

A Major Conundrum

As with so many other contentions of orthodox HIV/AIDS belief, however, this expectation is contrary to actual fact. The greatest risk of death from "HIV disease" comes at ages in the range of 35–45, just as at the beginning of the AIDS era. There was no dramatic increase in median age of death after 1996 following the adoption of HAART. . . .

This constitutes a major conundrum, a paradox: If HAART has extended life-spans by the claimed amounts, then why has not the median age of death increased dramatically? Why were so many AIDS patients still dying around age 45 in 2004?

The resolution of this conundrum is that the median ages of death are based on actually recorded deaths, whereas the claimed benefits of HAART were calculated on the basis of models incorporating many assumptions about the course of "HIV disease" and relying on contemporaneous death-rates. . . .

From 1996 to 1997, the annual numbers of deaths halved, and of course the percentage of deaths among survivors also halved. Since 1997, only between 2.8 and 5.7% of living "HIV/AIDS" patients have been dying annually, which is in keeping with the claims of life-saving benefits made for HAART on the basis of death rates and computer models. *But that conflicts with the age distribution of deaths, which has remained without major change during those same years.*

HIV Is Not a Causative Agent

If AIDS patients are now enjoying a virtually normal life-span, who are the people still dying at median age 45? If HAART is saving lives, why aren't those lives longer?

The reason is that testing "HIV-positive" is actually irrelevant to the cause of death. It does not indicate infection by a cause of illness, it is an indicator analogous to fever. Many conditions may stimulate a positive "HIV" test: vaccination against flu or tetanus, for example; or tuberculosis; or drug abuse; or pregnancy; and many more.

The likelihood that any given individual exposed to one of those conditions will actually test positive seems to correlate with the seriousness of the challenge to health; and it varies in a predictable manner with age, sex, and race. In any group of people, those who test "HIV-positive" are more likely to be or to become ill, so they are also more likely to die than those who do not test positive: just as in any group of people, those who have a fever are more likely to be ill and to die than those who do not have a fever. Also, of course, a fever does not necessarily presage death, nor does "HIV-positive" necessarily presage death; and in any group of people, some will die who never tested positive or who never had a fever. There's a strong correlation between illness, death, and fever, but it's not an inevitable one and fever is not the causative agent; there's a strong correlation between

Accepting No Responsibility

Funny how AIDS reappraisers who ask for transparency and dialogue, or warn of the shortcomings or dangers of HIV treatments are accused of causing unnecessary AIDS deaths. Strange that when someone dies after years of choosing not to take HIV drugs, fingers are immediately pointed at the AIDS denialists. And yet, when a patient dies after 2 or 6 or 12 years *on* HIV treatments, the AIDS Police speak of the extra few years treatment 'gave' the patient. Curiously, these self-described 'life-savers' accept no responsibility for those who died from high-dosage, experimental AZT [azidothymidine] monotherapy in the 1980s, or those whose entire skin 'detaches' while on AIDS drugs like Nevirapine.

Carl Stryg, "I Really, Really, Don't Care What Causes AIDS," The Truth Barrier *(blog), January 2010.* http://thetruthbarrier.com.

illness, death, and "HIV-positive", but it's not an inevitable one and "HIV" is not the causative agent.

So: Among people "living with HIV/AIDS", those who happen to die in any given year are simply ones whose "HIV-positive" status was associated with some actually life-threatening illness; and their ages were distributed just as ages are distributed in any group of "HIV-positive" people, with a median age at around 40, with minor variations depending on race and sex. For example, in 2000, there were more than 350,000 people "living with HIV/AIDS" whose median age was somewhere around 39.9. Of the 350,000 in 2000 with median age 39.9, 3.9% died; and the median age of those dying was 42.7. It's only to be expected, of course, that—among any group of people at all—those who die have a somewhat higher average age than those who don't die in that year.

The rate of death among "HIV/AIDS" patients declined markedly from 1987 to 1992 simply because "HIV/AIDS" was being increasingly defined to include illnesses less life-threatening than the original AIDS diseases of Kaposi's sarcoma and established opportunistic fungal infections. Another sharp drop in death rates came after 1992 when people who were not even ill came to be classed as "HIV/AIDS" patients and comprised about 70% of such patients. The last sudden drop in death rates, with the introduction of HAART in 1996, resulted not from any lifesaving benefit of HAART but because the latter superseded the earlier, much more toxic, high-dose regimens of AZT. The supposed benefits of HAART are to decrease viral load and allow CD4 counts to rise; but these effects come slowly and cannot explain a sudden improvement in clinical condition sufficient to bring a halving of deaths from one year to the next; on the other hand, stopping the administration of a highly toxic substance can certainly bring numbers of deaths down immediately. These data indicate, therefore, that something like half (at least) of "HIV/AIDS" deaths from 1987 through 1996—some 150,000—are attributable to the toxicity of AZT.

Through all those drastic as well as slower changes in death rates, among those "HIV/AIDS patients" who died for any one of a large variety of reasons, the median age of the "HIV-positive" ones remained about the same as it had always been. "HIV/AIDS" patients are not living longer despite the change in death rate from an annual 60% or more to 3% or less. . . .

The Reasoning Is Circular

This paradox follows "from the manner in which HIV tests were designed and from the fact that AIDS was defined in terms of 'HIV'". The genesis of the tests has been described lucidly by Neville Hodgkinson:

It never proved possible to validate the [*HIV*] tests by culturing, purifying and analysing particles of the purported virus from patients who test positive, then demonstrating that these are not present in patients who test negative. This was despite heroic efforts to make the virus reveal itself in patients with Aids [British style does not capitalize the acronym's letters] or at risk of Aids, in which their immune cells were stimulated for weeks in laboratory cultures using a variety of agents.

After the cells had been activated in this way, HIV pioneers found some 30 proteins in filtered material that gathered at a density characteristic of retroviruses. They attributed some of these to various parts of the virus. But they never demonstrated that these so-called 'HIV antigens' belonged to a new retrovirus. So, out of the 30 proteins, how did they select the ones to be defined as being from HIV? The answer is shocking, and goes to the root of what is probably the biggest scandal in medical history. They selected those that were most reactive with antibodies in blood samples from Aids patients and those at risk of Aids. This means that 'HIV' antigens are defined as such not on the basis of being shown to belong to HIV, but on the basis that they react with antibodies in Aids patients. Aids patients are then diagnosed as being infected with HIV on the basis that they have antibodies which react with those same antigens. The reasoning is circular.

"HIV" tests were created to react most strongly to substances present in the sera of very ill gay men whose average age was in the late 30s. That's why people who are in some manner health-challenged are more likely than others to test "HIV-positive", especially if they are aged around 40. Evidently the particular molecular species picked up by "HIV" tests are generated most prolifically around age 40, especially under the stimulation of various forms and degrees of physiological stress. That's why the median ages for testing "HIV-positive" and for being diagnosed with AIDS (criterion: positive HIV test) and for dying from

HIV/AIDS (criterion: positive HIV test) are all the same, in the range 35–45.

Perhaps some of what "HIV" tests detect are so-called "stress" or "heat-shock" proteins. That gay men so often test "HIV-positive" might have to do with molecular species associated with "leaky gut syndrome" or other consequences of intestinal dysbiosis.

Those are speculations, of course. What is not speculative, however, is that HAART does not prolong life even as it lowers death rates. It is also clear that testing "HIV-positive" is no more than an indicator of some form of physiological challenge, not necessarily infection by a pathogen and specifically not infection by a retrovirus that destroys the human immune system.

"Some [HIV] mutants are able to partly, or even fully, resist an antiretroviral drug."

HIV Drug Resistance Is a Concern

AIDS Community Research Initiative of America

Founded as the Community Research Initiative on AIDS in 1991, the AIDS Community Research Initiative of America (ACRIA) works toward community-based drug research and HIV awareness. In the following viewpoint, ACRIA states that drug resistance threatens the effectiveness of antiretrovirals. HIV replicates with many errors, creating mutant viruses, or variants, which may be resistant to a certain drug, ACRIA explains. Therefore, an antiretroviral regimen must include three or four drugs and be taken strictly as prescribed, ACRIA insists, to work against all of the variants present in the body and to prevent additional mutations.

As you read, consider the following questions:

1. What happens if a person infected with drug-resistant HIV takes antiretrovirals, according to the author?
2. What is cross-resistance, as described by ACRIA?

3. What happens when the trough level of an antiretroviral drug becomes too low, as reported by the author?

There are many types of germs, or pathogens, that can enter the human body. These include viruses, fungi, bacteria, and protozoa. Once inside the body, the primary goal of a germ is to survive and reproduce.

Pharmaceutical drugs are designed to target these germs and either kill them or prevent them from reproducing inside the body. If a germ continues to reproduce during treatment, it can change itself—or "mutate"—to avoid the drugs. This is called drug resistance.

When drug resistance occurs, the drug—or combination of drugs—loses its ability to block the germ from reproducing. Over time, the treatment can stop working completely. It is important to prevent germs from reproducing during treatment to prevent drug resistance from occurring.

How HIV Drug Resistance Occurs

Drug resistance occurs as a result of mutations in HIV's genetic structure, or genome. HIV's genome is in the form of RNA [ribonucleic acid], which the virus uses to produce more copies of itself.

Whenever a life form reproduces, mutations are possible. Human beings and other animals evolved into their present forms because of natural mutations that occurred over many thousands of years. Some mutations offer a survival advantage, and others make the life form less able to survive. This is what is meant by "survival of the fittest."

In order to prevent mutations from damaging our cells, our cells do a series of checks to make sure no mistakes have crept in during reproduction. The cells in our body are much more complex than HIV, and our body creates billions of them every day. In fact, every few years we have an almost entirely new body— almost all the cells in our body have died off and been replaced by new copies. But every new cell must have exactly the same DNA as the cells we were born with, or they could not function. Complex mechanisms are used to make sure that each of the 30,000 genes in our DNA is reproduced exactly.

HIV has only 9 genes and is too simple to have mechanisms to check for errors. So many errors routinely occur—and it is these errors that make it so difficult to control HIV. Mutations are very common in HIV. HIV reproduces at an extremely rapid rate and isn't able to correct mistakes made when its genetic material (RNA) is copied.

In order for antiretroviral drugs to be effective, they must first attach themselves to the enzyme they target, or interfere with a specific step of the HIV life cycle. Certain mutations can prevent a drug from binding with the enzyme and as a result make the drug less effective against the virus.

HIV drug-resistance mutations can occur both before and during therapy.

Mutations Before Therapy Begins

Mutations that occur before antiretroviral therapy is started can happen in two ways: natural selection and transmission of drug-resistant virus.

Natural selection: Soon after HIV enters the body, the virus begins reproducing at a rapid rate (up to 10 billion new viruses every day). Even if someone has been infected with HIV that is not resistant to any drugs, HIV makes both perfect copies of itself (wild-type virus) and copies containing errors (mutated virus). In fact, about 90% of the copies HIV makes of itself contain at least one mistake. These mutant viruses are called *variants*. Soon there is not just one type of virus in the body but, instead, a large population of mixed viruses called *quasi-species*.

Wild-type virus is the most natural and usually the "fittest" virus and, as a result, reproduces the best. Before antiretroviral therapy is started, wild-type virus is the most abundant in the body and dominates in the body. Some mutants are too weak to survive or cannot reproduce. Other mutants are strong enough to reproduce but still are not able to compete with the more "fit" wild-type virus. So, there is more wild-type virus than mutants in the body.

Some mutants are able to partly, or even fully, resist an antiretroviral drug. This is why people living with HIV should never take just one antiretroviral drug (monotherapy)—resistance can happen very quickly when taking just one drug, and sometimes because of just one mutation. HIV mutations occur randomly and there is no proven way to prevent them from occurring. Variants containing these mutations usually don't go on to develop additional mutations; doing so compromises their ability to stay alive in the body. So while these variants may be completely resistant to one antiretroviral drug, they are almost always sensitive to other drugs used in a regimen. This is why three-drug regimens work better: a variant may be resistant to one of the drugs but doesn't stand much of a chance when facing two other drugs that bind to different parts of the virus.

Transmission of drug-resistant virus: If someone who has taken antiretrovirals develops resistance to them and has unprotected sex or shares needles with someone who is not infected with the virus, it's possible that they can infect their partner with a drug-resistant variant—a strain of HIV containing mutations that causes resistance to one or more antiretroviral.

If a person is infected with resistant virus, the resistant virus would initially dominate all other viruses that are produced. Over time, wild-type virus will emerge and dominate. But this doesn't mean that the resistant virus is gone; it has merely become a minority member of the entire population of HIV. If the person starts therapy, even years later, the drugs would quickly control the wild-type HIV, but would probably be replaced with the resistant virus already in the body. As a result, the person might have a difficult time reducing viral load or keeping it undetectable.

According to some studies, between 10% and 30% of all new HIV infections (defined variously as people infected with HIV over the past three years) involve strains resistant to at least one antiretroviral drug or class of drugs. A recent study found that 3% of new HIV infections had resistance to all three classes of antiretrovirals, while other studies showed as many as 11% of new infections being resistant to more than one drug. Resistance to the non-nucleoside reverse transcriptase inhibitors was most common. Researchers expect these rates to increase in the years to come.

It might also be possible for someone who is already infected with HIV to be infected, again, with a (multiple) drug-resistant strain of HIV. This is sometimes referred to as *reinfection* or *superinfection*. There have now been several reports demonstrating that this is possible, although there is still debate as to how often this occurs in people who have had HIV for longer than a year.

Mutations During Therapy

Before antiretroviral therapy is begun, wild-type virus dominates and while there are some mutants, they are far fewer in number and will not usually show up on a resistance test.

Soon after antiretroviral therapy is started, the amount of both wild-type and mutant virus in the body is reduced dramatically. Unfortunately, no antiretroviral drug—or combination of drugs—is able to completely stop HIV from reproducing. In other words, there is always a small population of virus in the body that continues reproducing, despite the presence of antiretroviral [drugs].

Wild-type virus is the most sensitive to antiretroviral drugs. Because of this, HIV mutants in the body have a survival advantage over wild-type virus once anti-HIV drugs are taken. If antiretroviral drugs are not able to completely suppress HIV, mutants can become the dominant strain of HIV.

If a person with resistant virus stops all antiretrovirals, their viral population will soon revert to a state that [first appeared]. In reality, however, the resistant virus created earlier still exists, and will quickly reappear once the person restarts HAART [highly active antiretroviral therapy]. This is why resistance testing is best done while on medication.

Resistant virus usually persists for life, and once an individual becomes resistant to a drug, that drug will most likely never be useful for that person again.

Over time, variants accumulate additional mutations. Some of these mutations will harm the virus while others will further limit a drug's ability to stop it from reproducing. Once the virus has accumulated enough mutations, the antiretroviral drugs lose their ability to bind to it and prevent it from reproducing. As the drugs become weaker, the amount of drug-resistant virus in the body increases, causing an undetectable viral load to become detectable again and increase over time. Should the drug-resistant virus continue to reproduce, it can acquire even more mutations to resist the antiretroviral drugs completely. But, as mentioned earlier, sometimes a single mutation can lead to complete resistance against a drug.

Mutations that emerge during therapy can be divided into two groups: *primary mutations* and *secondary mutations*. Each antiretroviral drug is associated with at least one primary mutation. This mutation is of greatest concern, as they are the ones that cause the greatest amount of drug resistance. Secondary mutations do not cause drug resistance unless a primary mutation is present. If both primary and secondary mutations are present, drug resistance can become more complicated.

While primary and secondary mutations can cause the virus to become resistant to anti-HIV drugs, they usually have a negative effect on the power of the virus. This is why some people who are experiencing an increase in their viral load might not see a decrease in their CD4+ cell counts, at least not at first. In other words, the virus loses its ability to cause damage to the immune system if it contains drug-resistance mutations. However, some studies show that certain primary and secondary mutations can cause the virus to regain its power and, quite possibly, become even more powerful than wild-type virus. In turn, most experts recommend switching therapies before the virus accumulates any additional mutations.

Cross-resistance can also occur during therapy. When HIV becomes resistant to one drug, it can automatically become resistant to other drugs in the same class. For example, the K103N mutation seen in some people's virus after taking [the antiretroviral drug brand] Sustiva can automatically cause that virus also to be resistant to both Viramune and Rescriptor [brands]. Even if the person hasn't yet taken Viramune or Rescriptor, he or she will likely be cross-resistant to the drug and will not likely benefit from it.

The key to avoiding the accumulation of mutations that cause resistance and cross-resistance is to keep the amount of virus in the body as low as possible, for as long as possible.

Accumulating Resistant Mutants

Don't forget the golden rule: the less virus there is in the body, the less likely it is that the virus will continue reproducing and mutating. A powerful antiretroviral regimen is the most effective way to keep the level of virus low—preferably undetectable (<50 copies/mL)—and to delay additional mutations from occurring.

Monotherapy (taking just one anti-HIV drug—the standard until the early '90s) didn't work because it lowered viral loads by only 70%. This left 30% of the virus in the body to mutate and become resistant, usually within a very short period of time. Taking two drugs lowered viral loads by 90–95%, but resistance still emerged. In most people, three or even four drugs are needed, since a three-drug combination can lower viral loads up to 99.9%. If virus levels can be kept that low, a combination could work for many years.

There are a number of factors that can prevent an antiretroviral drug regimen from being as powerful as it can be. These include:

Poor adherence or compliance. In order for antiretroviral drugs to work correctly, they must be taken exactly as prescribed.

This means taking the correct number of pills each day, being careful to take them a certain number of hours apart, while at the same time following dietary requirements (see "poor absorption" below).

Skipping doses or not taking medication correctly can cause the *trough level* of an antiretroviral drug to decrease in the body. The trough level refers to the amount of drug left in a person's body just before another dose of the drug is taken by mouth. If the trough level becomes too low, there may still be enough drug in the body to control wild-type HIV (which is most sensitive to the drugs), but not enough to control the variants. If the variants are able to keep reproducing, they will soon outnumber wild-type virus and become the dominant virus in the body.

According to a few research reports, a person with HIV must be more than 95% adherent with his or her antiretroviral drug regimen in order for it to continue working properly. This means missing less than one dose a month.

Poor absorption. Not only must antiretroviral drugs be taken on schedule, they also need to be absorbed effectively into the bloodstream. A drug that is not absorbed properly can result in trough levels that are too low and, ultimately, allow HIV reproduction and the accumulation of drug-resistance mutations.

Some drugs have specific dietary requirements. For example, people taking [the drug brand] Videx shouldn't eat anything 1/2 hour before or 2 hours after taking it. Conversely, Prezista should be taken with a meal, or within two hours of a meal. If dietary requirements are not followed while taking any of these drugs, drug levels in the body will decrease.

People with HIV can also experience diarrhea and vomiting. These can cause antiretroviral drugs to be expelled from the gut too quickly, reducing the amount of drug absorbed into the bloodstream.

Varying pharmacokinetics. Pharmacokinetics is a term used by researchers to describe how a drug is absorbed, distributed, metabolized, and removed from the body. Pharmacokinetics are measured by checking drug levels in blood that is drawn over various periods of time.

Even though two people might receive the exact same dose of a drug, the amount of drug may be higher in one person's bloodstream than in the others. Factors that can contribute to this difference include their body weight, height, and age. Some people process, or metabolize, drugs faster or slower than others do. This can speed up—or slow down—the rate at which a drug is cleared from the body.

It is important to remember that a drug's correct dose, as approved by the FDA [Food and Drug Administration], is determined in clinical trials based on the average dose found to be safe and effective. In other words, some people may be able to keep their viral load undetectable using lower doses of the drug, while some people might require higher doses of the drug to keep their viral load undetectable. Healthcare providers can perform blood tests to measure the amount of drug in their patients' bodies. This is called *therapeutic drug monitoring* (TDM) and it may help determine whether or not a person has a correct trough level of each medication to ensure that viral load remains low or undetectable.

| "Studies . . . have shown that micronutrients act to control HIV infection and AIDS."

Nutritional AIDS Treatments Are Effective

Raxit J. Jariwalla, Aleksandra Niedzwiecki, and Matthias Rath

In the following viewpoint, Raxit J. Jariwalla, Aleksandra Niedzwiecki, and Matthias Rath suggest that nutritional supplements can more effectively control HIV infection and AIDS than antiretroviral drugs. The authors claim that micronutrients suppress the multiplication and spread of the virus, restore immune responses, and slow the progression of AIDS. For example, South African AIDS patients that received a combination of nutritional supplements saw major improvements in weight loss and other symptoms without the side effects of conventional drug treatment. Raxit J. Jariwalla is senior researcher at the Dr. Rath Health Foundation, established by physician Matthias Rath as a nonprofit organization advocating natural health care. Aleksandra Niedzwiecki is a board member of the foundation and vice president of research at Matthias Rath, Inc.

Raxit J. Jariwalla, Ph.D., Aleksandra Niedzwiecki, Ph.D., and Matthias Rath, MD , "Role of Micronutrients in the Control of HIV and AIDS," *Commonwealth Health Ministers Book 2007*. Copyright © 2007 by Commonwealth Secretariat. All rights reserved. Reproduced by permission.

As you read, consider the following questions:

1. In the authors' opinion, what are the limitations of antiretroviral drugs?
2. According to Jariwalla, Niedzwiecki, and Rath, what was one of the first vitamins thought to play a role in immunity?
3. What is the critical role of vitamin C, as stated by the authors?

A IDS has become a global health crisis and a leading cause of death in the developing world. Since 1981, more than 25 million people worldwide have died from this immunodeficiency syndrome and 12 million AIDS orphans have been left behind in Africa alone. According to the UNAIDS/World Health Organization (WHO) 2006 AIDS epidemic update, the number of people living with HIV (human immunodeficiency virus), the virus linked to AIDS, has grown from 8 million in 1990 to nearly 40 million at the end of 2006. Despite improvements in access to antiretroviral (ARV) drugs, the death toll from AIDS in 2006 was close to 3 million, indicating the need for alternative/complementary therapeutic modalities.

AIDS Characteristics and Causality

AIDS is characterised by progressive depletion of a specific group of immune cells called (CD4+) helper T lymphocytes whose loss leads to opportunistic infections and cancer. Since 1983, AIDS has been linked to infection by HIV, which primarily infects CD4+ T cells. Several mechanisms have been proposed for the depletion of CD4+ cells that include: direct cytolysis [cell disruption] by HIV, defective T cell regeneration, immune unresponsiveness and T cell death [apoptosis]. Although HIV has been correlated with AIDS, the virus infects only a small proportion of CD4 cells and T cell apoptosis occurs primarily in uninfected bystander cells, suggesting the involvement of other factors.

Very early in the AIDS epidemic, it was recognised that protein calorie malnutrition and specific micronutrient deficiencies were common in HIV and AIDS patients. Since micronutrients are essential for immune function, nutritional abnormalities can impair immune-cell production and play an important role in AIDS development.

Limitations of Current Treatment

Conventional treatment is based on the use of ARV drugs directed against HIV. Although ARVs can lower HIV level in the blood, they can neither restore the immune system nor cure AIDS. Effectiveness of ARVs also wears out with time and the drugs are expensive and not readily accessible in developing countries. Most importantly, ARV drugs are highly toxic to the bone marrow as well as other organs including heart, muscle, liver, and nerves. Consequently, ARVs can further weaken the immune system and pose a potential risk for AIDS development.

Two uncontrolled surveys of the effects of anti-HIV drugs on asymptomatic HIV-positive patients, one conducted in the USA and another in Canada, reported mortality rates from AIDS of 8.8% and 6.7% respectively. These surveys did not determine AIDS mortality in drug-free controls. However, the global AIDS development rate for all HIV-positive persons in the world (only a minority of whom took ARV drugs) was estimated by the WHO to be 1.4% for the year 2000, which fell between that of the above two surveys. Assuming that everyone who developed AIDS in 2000 died in the same year, the global AIDS mortality rate would still be 1.4%, which is 4- to 6-fold lower than the 6.7–8.8 per cent rate reported in the Canadian and US surveys for HIV-positive people on ARV drugs. Hence, ARV drugs could pose a potential risk for AIDS development in HIV-positive people. A more recent study of HIV patients in Singapore reported that malnutrition at the time of starting ARV treatment was significantly associated with reduced survival, indicating the need for nutritional therapy to effectively combat AIDS.

Essential Micronutrients

Vitamins and minerals are essential for sustaining life. Their role in building cellular structures, generating biological energy and acting as biocatalysts of multiple enzymatic processes in the body are well documented in the textbooks of biochemistry and cell biology.

Although vitamins, minerals and trace elements are required in much smaller quantities than proteins, fats or sugars, without them none of the food component can be utilised in cellular metabolism. Suboptimal micronutrient intake is not easy to detect because our body has not developed clear warning signals for their deficiencies such as the ones alerting us about shortages in oxygen (suffocation), water (thirst) and food (hunger). Research has shown that individual requirements for particular vitamins or minerals vary, depending on many factors such as one's genetics, age, health status, environment and other factors. In some cases micronutrient intakes well above the average levels recommended for the general public (RDA) can alleviate various pathological conditions.

Nutrition and Immunity

Close interrelationship between nutrition and resistance to infections has been recognised since the early 20th century. Analysis of trends in mortality during the last 150 years has shown that decline in death caused by infectious diseases, commonly attributed to development of antibiotics and modern medical technology, was actually occurring long prior to emergence of these technologies and was related to improved nutrition, better food supply and sanitation.

One of the first vitamins recognised for its role in immunity was vitamin A, which was even named an 'anti-infective' vitamin. However, the discovery of sulfa antibiotics around that time led to about 50 years of neglect in clinical investigation of this and other vitamins in various aspects of infections.

Micronutrients as HIV Therapy

Micronutrient(s)	Clinical Improvement Seen
Vitamins C (1500 mg daily) and E (600 IU daily)	Lowered oxidative stress and viral load
Vitamins C and E	Prevented damage to muscle cell mitochondria induced by AZT
N-acetyleysteine (NAC)	Conferred statistically significant survival advantage over placebo
High dose NAC and Vitamin C	Improved immune responses and lowered viral load in patients with advanced AIDS
Multivitamin (B-complex, C and E) supplements	Significantly reduced risks of adverse pregnancy outcomes including fetal death among HIV-infected women in Tanzania
Multivitamin supplements	Improved mortality among HIV-infected individuals living in Bangkok [Thailand]
Broad-spectrum micronutrient supplement	Improved CD4 count in HIV-infected persons on ARV therapy

Raxit J. Jariwalla, Aleksandra Niedzwiecki, and Matthias Rath, Commonwealth Health Ministers Book, *2007.*

It is well documented that clinical and sub-clinical micronutrient deficiency and infections are mutually aggravating, as infections can turn even marginal micronutrient deficiencies into severe conditions, and vice versa—namely, micronutrient deficiencies can increase susceptibility to infections. Most vitamins, such as vitamin A, vitamin C, B-group vitamins, vitamin D and E support the production of white blood cells, as well as various cytokines and cellular modulators of immunity, including antibody production. Among other important biological factors impacting immunity at cellular and organ levels are availability of minerals, such as iron, copper, magnesium, selenium and zinc.

A Universal Problem

Today, insufficient intake of micronutrients has become a universal problem recognised by various international organisations, including the UN organisation UNICEF [United Nations Children's Fund], which stated in a recent document that about 2 billion people worldwide suffer from vitamin and mineral deficiencies, "debilitating minds, bodies, energies and the economic prospects of nations". This problem is not limited exclusively to the developing countries. Sub-optimal intakes of micronutrients are also frequent in the industrialised world as a result of modern farming technologies, food transportation, storage and processing. However, even though micronutrient deficiencies have been officially acknowledged as a worldwide problem and the solutions for that are easily available and economically viable, they are not being implemented.

Micronutrients and Health

The last decade has expanded our understandings of the role of vitamins, minerals and other nutrients beyond supporting immune system function at the cellular level. Some micronutrients are important as direct modulators of viral and bacterial metabolism and in controlling the spread of infections in the body. Among them vitamin C and the amino acids lysine and proline are critical in strengthening natural biological barriers surrounding our body cells, thereby curtailing spread of viruses and other infectious agents. Vitamin C, N-acetylcysteine (NAC) and green tea polyphenols can also suppress the multiplication of viruses directly or decrease their infectivity. This new cellular medicine approach is based on micronutrient synergy rather than individual components and their random combinations. Clinical applications of specifically selected micronutrient combinations acting in biological synergy have been proven effective in various pathological conditions.

Micronutrients Can Control AIDS

AIDS is the major health problem linked to malnutrition and micronutrient deficiency. Research in cellular medicine has revealed that micronutrients can modify the course of viral infection and restore the functionality of the immune system in a nontoxic fashion. Studies conducted with both single and multiple nutritional supplements have shown that micronutrients act to control HIV infection and AIDS in three specific ways, which include: (i) suppression of virus multiplication and spread; (ii) restoration of cell-mediated immune responses and (iii) slowing the rate of AIDS progression and reducing the severity of AIDS-defining and disease-related symptoms.

Suppression of HIV by Nutrients

Experimental studies using laboratory cultures of HIV-infected cells have demonstrated that specific micronutrients can block virus multiplication or expression at different stages of infection. These nutrients include vitamin C, NAC, alpha-lipoic acid, selenium and Epigallocatechin gallate (EGCG), a flavanoid from green tea. Micronutrients such as NAC, lipoic acid, and vitamin C have been shown to have immune-enhancing or stabilising effects on T cells. A broad-spectrum micronutrient combination was shown recently to elevate CD4 cell count in HIV-infected subjects on ARV therapy.

Additional Benefits

In addition to virus-suppressing and immune-modulating effects, micronutrient supplements have been reported to confer benefits to HIV-infected subjects in clinical studies. . . .

More recently, the effects of a defined micronutrient programme on the course of AIDS symptoms in HIV-positive patients was evaluated as part of a community-based nutritional health programme led by the South African National Civic Organization (SANCO) in the Khayelitsha township outside of Cape Town. Participants included 100 adult HIV positive men and non-pregnant women with advanced AIDS symptoms without current or recent use of ARV drugs. After meeting eligibility requirements and providing informed consent, participants took a nutritional supplement (supplied in the form of tablets) consisting of a defined combination of vitamins, minerals, trace elements, amino acids, and polyphenols (from green tea) among other nutrients. Before taking the supplement (0 weeks) and after periodic visits (5 weeks and 12 weeks), a licensed physician examined the participants and assessed their health status using a questionnaire. The latter was graded on a scale of 0 to 4 to assess AIDS-defining symptoms and other physical symptoms (0 = no symptoms, 1 = mild, 2 = medium, 3 = advanced, 4 = severe). . . .

The data showed a substantial reduction after only a few weeks in severity of fever, weight loss, diarrhoea, cough and TB [tuberculosis] symptoms that constitute the five key symptoms for WHO's case definition of AIDS based on a conference in Bangui, Central Africa. In addition, the severity of fungal and opportunistic infections accompanying AIDS in nine participants were also lower after micronutrient intake. All these changes were statistically significant. Significant reduction was also seen in other physical symptoms associated with AIDS such as wounds, sores, skin rashes, swollen glands, fatigue, colds, etc. Micronutrient supplements also mediated healing of skin ulcers. No adverse side effects were seen from intake of the micronutrient supplements.

Implications in HIV/AIDS

The results from micronutrient supplementation studies have implications for further research and adoption of nutritional therapy into public health programmes of developing countries. Specifically, micronutrient supplementation offers a safe, effective and affordable therapeutic option that may provide benefits to HIV-infected people, especially undernourished populations with a background of malnutrition. Micronutrients lowered in HIV infection have been shown to affect cell-mediated immune responses and to influence the rate of AIDS progression. Hence, nutrient supplementation may offer an opportunity for early intervention in HIV, thereby delaying the start of (toxic) ARV therapy.

"*[Nutritional AIDS therapy promoter
Matthias] Rath must be arrested as he
carries responsibility for the death of
my wife and many other people.*"

Nutritional AIDS Treatments Are Quackery

Anso Thom

*In the following viewpoint, Anso Thom alleges that Matthias Rath,
a German vitamin seller, marketed ineffective and dangerous nutritional supplements to South Africans desperate for an HIV cure.
Thom says that Rath recruited HIV-positive people for clinical trials to test the effectiveness of his supplements. Consequently, two
women with HIV died within weeks of starting Rath's regimen of
high-dose vitamins, insists the author, and Rath and his team left
without explanation to the families and took no responsibility.
Thom is a journalist for the Health-e News Service in South Africa
and coeditor of* The Virus, Vitamins & Vegetables: The South
African HIV/AIDS Mystery.

As you read, consider the following questions:

1. What happened after Noluthando Magwebu began taking
   pills from the Rath Foundation, as stated by Thom?

2. How long did it take for the government to halt Rath's clinical trials and investigate him, according to the author?

3. As reported by Thom, what did Rath Foundation agents advise Norah Sigebenga to do if she felt ill when taking the vitamins?

Zondani Magwebu bites his lower lip and stares out the front door of his one-roomed house in Khayelitsha's Kuyasa neighbourhood. Dusk is settling over the dusty street outside his green-painted house and high pitched shrieks of playing children pierce the early evening calm.

A stout middle-aged man, Magwebu's mouth forms the words he strings together, but his eyes express the pain, confusion and anger that has settled over his family since the death of his wife, Noluthando.

The Magwebu family's story appeared in the *Cape Times* in September 2005 when Zondani, who opted to remain anonymous then, shared the circumstances that had left their three children without a mother and him devastated.

At the time, Magwebu revealed details of how agents working for discredited German vitamin seller Matthias Rath's foundation arrived at his home asking to see Noluthando, who had earlier been diagnosed HIV positive.

An Alternative to HIV Drugs

Rath had arrived in South Africa in 2004 and, with the help of community organizations such as the South African National Civic Organisation (Sanco), vigorously marketed his Vita Cell multivitamins as an alternative to antiretrovirals. Khayelitsha was one of his main targets.

Magwebu said doctors had told Noluthando that she did not yet need antiretroviral drugs but the young woman had been receiving prophylactic [preventive] treatment to ward off tuberculosis and pneumonia as well as multi-vitamins from the local clinic. "She had ulcers, but that was it," he recalled.

He said that the two Rath women, who were also members of Sanco, convinced his wife that the Rath Foundation's pills "would make the HIV much better".

"She was told to take 10 tablets in the morning and 10 in the evening. The day after she had started taking it she became very dizzy and incoherent. She vomited and became weaker and weaker. We took her to the (government) clinic where the doctor advised her to not take the Rath medicine, but to rather continue with her other medication," said Magwebu.

Magwebu says he is convinced that she didn't stop taking the pills as he worked long hours and could not monitor her medication. Her condition continued to deteriorate. She died within three weeks in GF Jooste Hospital's medical ward.

So-Called Clinics and Trials

With the help of Sanco, Rath had managed to set up so-called clinics in 2005 and was openly sharing details of the "clinical trials" he had been conducting in Khayelitsha. Reports were surfacing of HIV positive people desperate for a "cure" who had been easily persuaded to take the Rath vitamins in the place of antiretrovirals or prophylactic medication, which keeps life-threatening infections at bay.

The Treatment Action Campaign challenged Rath on several occasions in court, but it would take four long years before the courts would finally order that the German stop conducting any further trials and that government investigate his activities.

National Health Department Director General Thami Mseleku had claimed on several occasions that the government was busy investigating Rath and found no reason to prosecute him. However, it was subsequently revealed in court that the "investigation" had involved two telephone calls, both to Rath employees.

No Dissent

Despite the extremes of this case, not one single alternative therapist or nutritionist, anywhere in the world, has stood up to criticise any single aspect of the activities of Matthias Rath and his colleagues. In fact, far from it: he continues to be fêted to this day. I have sat in true astonishment and watched leading figures of the UK's alternative therapy movement applaud Matthias Rath at a public lecture (I have it on video, just in case there's any doubt). Natural health organisations continue to defend Rath. Homeopaths' mailouts continue to promote his work. The British Association of Nutritional Therapists has been invited to comment by bloggers, but declined. Most, when challenged, will dissemble. "Oh," they say, "I don't really know much about it." Not one person will step forward and dissent.

Ben Goldacre, Bad Science, *2009.*

Magwebu confirms that no one ever contacted him to try and establish the circumstances around Nolunthando's death. "Nobody has been here to try and explain to me what happened or to just hear my story," he said.

Visiting Magwebu on the eve of World Aids Day 2008, he is a shadow of the man Health-e interviewed in 2005. He looks tired and gaunt, he doesn't smile easily and appears pensive and worried.

The tiny house, which had been lovingly decorated by Noluthando, is now a bare structure with two wooden benches, a non-functioning fridge in one corner and a kitchen area in the other.

The smell of burning porridge hangs thick in the air as Magwebu's eldest, Bulelani (14), stirs a dented pot of porridge over a two-plate stove. His sister Landiswa (11) plays with a skipping rope across the road while little Asiphe (5) lurks nearby.

"Since my wife moved on, things have been bad here," he sighs, staring at the floor.

"It is increasingly difficult for me to look after the children. I am working as a builder, but while I am away things go wrong at home, things go wrong at school and I am not coping. It has been difficult."

Magwebu is clear that Noluthando would have still been alive if she hadn't taken the high doses of vitamins that she had been advised to take by the Rath agents. "It is very, very difficult for me to think about how it could have been. It is very difficult for the youngest one, for Asiphe. She needs her mother. The older ones are able to look after themselves.

"They try to cook, but they're not the greatest cooks," says Magwebu, flashing a rare smile.

"Their mother would have sorted things out, but I can't help, I worry about the little one all the time."

Asked about his own health, Magwebu pauses: "I am feeling okay. Health wise I am okay, but I worry a lot. I worry about work. I am a builder and at the moment I have no work. The kids have no clothes to wear. Christmas is coming and I have nothing to give them.

"I have not been for a (health) check-up for a long time, but I think I am okay."

"Tablets Are Not an Option"

Magwebu then leans forward and says: "I can definitely tell you. I for one will not take any tablets. I don't trust tablets anymore. I saw what happened to my wife. If I ever had to fall ill, they will have to give me an injection, but tablets are not an option.

"I do acknowledge that the tablets they (Rath agents) gave her were wrong, but I cannot get myself to take tablets. I am confused. At the moment I also cannot think of going to a clinic. I guess if I become really ill for one reason or another in the future I will force myself to go, but for now I can't think of that."

Asked whether he held any grudges, Magwebu nods: "I don't want to lie to you. I know there is very little I can do, but I do wish I could lay charges. Rath must be arrested as he carries responsibility for the death of my wife and many other people."

Magwebu feels that the government needs to take some responsibility. "Of course I am living in a country where I cannot take the law into my own hands, but I do feel that government needs to be held accountable for what happened here. Maybe someone else can charge government, because I don't think I can. If government knew what was happening and they did nothing, they need to be held accountable.

"When I think of the future it gets tricky for me. Sometimes I think I need to find a companion, but it has its own complications. Perhaps the children need someone, especially the girls. They need a woman in the house. I sometimes get confused about what the right thing is to do. With Bulelani it is fine, I know what to do.

"I can tell you, this thing is in my head all the time."

Another Victim

Diagonally across the road from Magwebu, a light shines through the single window at the front of house 56202. Inside, Nandipha Sigebenga sits on a single bed which serves the dual purpose of couch in the day and bed at night for her four daughters and grandchild.

A poster mounted above the bed dominates the front part of the tiny house, proclaiming: "I wish a long life to all my enemies so they may see all my successes."

In 2005 Sigebenga, who also opted to remain anonymous then, shared the horror story of her younger sister Norah's death.

She had just returned from burying her sister in the Cofimvaba in the Eastern Cape. At the time she was unequivocal that when the two Rath women arrived at their home, they handed Norah her death certificate.

Norah, a security guard, had been sickly for some time and had been treated for various infections, including tuberculosis.

On March 16, Norah arrived home and told Sigebenga that two women had introduced her to new medication. "She said that they were going to observe her for two months and that she would get better," said Sigebenga.

The women took her to a Sanco-Rath clinic in Site C. "She was told to strip down and she was photographed from various angles. She also told me that they put her on a drip for the whole day. When she got home, I could see her face and hands were swollen. She had to take 14 tablets every day," Sigebenga said at the time.

"She was dizzy. She would vomit. She grew weak, she lost her appetite and she told me she was losing her senses. She couldn't even go to the toilet," Sigebenga recalled through tears.

Sigebenga still stands by her claims that Matthias Rath personally visited their house when her sister grew distressed over the fact that she was not getting better and demanded to see a doctor.

"He sat in that chair," says a resolute Sigebenga, pointing at a chair next to the front door.

"My sister was really sick, but he told me she was fine and that their pills would soon take effect," she says.

One night, three weeks after starting on the vitamins, Norah vomited non-stop but believed that this was a sign that her body was being cleansed of the disease. When Sigebenga called an ambulance, Thandi refused to get into it. She told her sister that she had been instructed by the Rath women not to go to hospital but to visit their clinic in an emergency.

A few hours later she was dead. Five hours after her death, one of the Rath women arrived and without asking for permission or offering her condolences, she removed all the medication, even the empty containers, erasing any traces of Norah's treatment.

Nowhere to Be Seen

A tall, no-nonsense woman, Sigebenga's eyes mist over behind her black-framed spectacles: "I try to close this chapter, but it is not easy. It has taken me two years to get back on track again and it's hard for me to think she is gone, sometimes I think it's all just a horrible nightmare and she will walk through the front door again."

"Now you can go into the streets and there is no trace of any of those people who used to work for Rath. They are nowhere to be seen. Strangely enough, I have forgiven them. Even if Rath had to come to my house I would invite him in."

She grows animated as she continues: "But I would have some questions for him. I will ask him—'When you went around giving people these tablets, did you know it was killing people, destroying their lives?' This is what I want to know."

"I know Manto (former Health Minister Dr Manto Tshabalala-Msimang) spoke about garlic and all those things at the time, but I find it absolutely shocking that they might have known what Rath was up to. I ask myself how they could have allowed him to do this to us."

Sigebenga says she longs for closure, but that it has been hard to find it with nobody attempting to answer their burning questions.

She walks to the back of her house and returns with a photograph of chubby, smiling boy in khaki pants and a t-shirt: "One day I will have to tell Norah's son what happened to his mother. What do I tell him? It is not easy to find these answers," she sighs.

"He looks to me for the answers and right now, I don't have those answers."

Rath finally left South Africa in 2006 and according to reports he has now turned his sights on Russia. Another Rath ally, the Traditional Healers Organisation continues to distribute Rath Foundation booklets in KwaZulu-Natal with unconfirmed reports that patients are still reporting to government clinics having been offered Rath's Vita Cell.

Periodical and Internet Sources Bibliography

The following articles have been selected to supplement the diverse views presented in this chapter.

Françoise Barre-Sinoussi	"Toward an HIV Cure," *New York Times*, June 3, 2011.
Misti Crane	"After 30 Years, Hope Exists for HIV Cure," *Columbus Dispatch*, June 5, 2011.
Celia Farber	"Over the Rainbow with Marco Ruggiero," *The Truth Barrier* January 24, 2011. www .thetruthbarrier.com.
Margie Mason and Martha Mendoza	"South African Doctor Sees Drug-Resistant HIV," Associated Press, December 31, 2009. www.ap.org.
Bob Roehr	"Giving HIV a Poor Reception: New AIDS Treatment Tinkers with Immune Cell Genes," *Scientific American*, March 3, 2011.
Tina Rosenberg	"The Man Who Had HIV and Now Does Not," *New York Magazine*, May 29, 2011.
Mark Schoofs	"A Doctor, a Mutation and a Potential Cure for AIDS," *Wall Street Journal*, November 7, 2008.
Sonia Smith	"Fighting AIDS in Tanzania," *Slate*, June 9, 2011. www.slate.com.
Anso Thom	"Charting a New Course for HIV and TB," Health-e News Service, June 10, 2011. www.health-e .org.za.
Sarah Zaidi	"Differential Treatment: Restricted Access to Newer Antiretrovirals," *UN Chronicle*, May 15, 2011.

For Further Discussion

Chapter 1

1. Jonny Steinberg and Henry Bauer both draw on scientific evidence to support their arguments that HIV does and does not cause AIDS, respectively. In your view, who provides the more valid evidence? Use examples from the viewpoints to explain your answer.

Chapter 2

1. Michael Fitzpatrick maintains that AIDS organizations and advocacy groups exaggerate the global AIDS epidemic. In your view, should the claims of AVERT, as an AIDS charity, be scrutinized? Why or why not?

2. Stephanie Nolen speculates that the statistic of 28 million Africans infected with HIV is low compared to her own experiences and those working in stricken areas. In your opinion, does Nolen's speculation reinforce Matthew Cullinan Hoffman's claim that HIV/AIDS statistics for Africa are overblown? Why or why not?

Chapter 3

1. David McQuoid-Mason suggests that routine HIV testing in democratic nations further justifies its enforcement. Do you agree or disagree with McQuoid-Mason? Why or why not?

Chapter 4

1. Sten H. Vermund declares that antiretroviral drugs save the lives of those infected with HIV. In your opinion, does Henry Bauer successfully counter Vermund's position? Cite examples from the texts to support your response.

2. In your opinion, does the AIDS Community Research Initiative of America provide a satisfactory explanation

for drug resistance in HIV patients? Why or why not?

3. Anso Thom claims that Matthias Rath abandoned Africa after AIDS patients died while taking his vitamin regimen. In your view, does Thom's investigation damage the positive outcomes reported in the opposing viewpoint by Rath and colleagues? Why or why not?

Organizations to Contact

The editors have compiled the following list of organizations concerned with the issues debated in this book. The descriptions are derived from materials provided by the organizations. All have publications or information available for interested readers. The list was compiled on the date of publication of the present volume; names, addresses, phone and fax numbers, and e-mail and Internet addresses may change. Be aware that many organizations take several weeks or longer to respond to inquiries, so allow as much time as possible.

AIDS Community Research Initiative of America (ACRIA)
230 W. 38th Street, 17th Floor
New York, New York 10018
(212) 924-3934
website: www.acria.org

ACRIA was founded as the Community Research Initiative on AIDS (CRIA) in December 1991 by a group of physicians, activists, and people living with HIV who were frustrated by the slow pace of government and academic AIDS research. ACRIA has contributed to the development of more than a dozen medications that have received approval by the US Food and Drug Administration.

AIDS Vaccine Advocacy Coalition (AVAC)
432 W. 127th Street, 4th Floor
New York, NY 10027
(212) 796-6423
e-mail: avac@avac.org
website: www.avac.org

AVAC is a community- and consumer-based organization founded in 1995 to accelerate the ethical development and global delivery of vaccines for HIV/AIDS. The organization provides independent analysis, policy advocacy, public education, and mobilization to enhance AIDS research. It also provides various reports and publications.

Alive and Well AIDS Alternatives

11684 Ventura Blvd.
Studio City, California 91604
(818) 780-1875 • fax: (818) 780-7093
e-mail: info@aliveandwell.org
website: www.aliveandwell.org

Alive and Well AIDS Alternatives is an organization that presents information that questions the validity of many of the common assumptions about HIV and AIDS, including the accuracy of HIV tests and the effectiveness of AIDS drug treatments. The organization's website features information on whether a link exists between HIV and AIDS and also addresses facts and myths about AIDS drugs.

American Foundation for AIDS Research (amfAR)

120 Wall Street, 13th Floor
New York, New York 10005-3908
(212) 806-1600 • fax: (212) 806-1601
website: www.amfar.org

AmfAR is a nonprofit organization that supports HIV/AIDS research, treatment education, and AIDS prevention. Its mission is to prevent HIV infection and to protect the human rights of everyone who is affected by the epidemic. The organization publishes an electronic newsletter, reports on HIV/AIDS in Asia and the Pacific, an annual report, and several issue briefs.

AVERT

4 Brighton Road, Horsham West
Sussex, United Kingdom RH13 5BA
+44 (0)1403 210202
website: www.avert.org

AVERT provides a wide range of information to educate people about HIV/AIDS across the world. With over two hundred pages, AVERT's website describes all aspects of HIV and AIDS as well as specific areas for young people, interactive quizzes, an extensive photo gallery, and videos. Its Community Program supports and builds partnerships with local organizations that work directly to avert the spread of HIV and AIDS and to improve treatment, care, and support.

Center for Women Policy Studies (CWPS)
1776 Massachusetts Ave. NW, Suite 450
Washington, DC 20036
(202) 872-1770 • fax: (202) 296-8962
e-mail: cwps@centerwomenpolicy.org
website: www.centerwomenpolicy. org

The CWPS was the first national policy institute to focus specifically on issues affecting the social, legal, and economic status of women. CWPS believes that the government and the medical community have neglected the effect of AIDS on women and that more action should be taken to help women who have AIDS.

Centers for Disease Control and Prevention (CDC)
National Prevention Information Network (NPIN)
PO Box 6003
Rockville, MD 20849-6003
(800) 458-5231 • fax: (888) 282-7681
e-mail: info@cdcnpin.org
website: www.cdcnpin.org

The CDC is the government agency charged with protecting the public health by preventing and controlling diseases and by responding to public health emergencies. It publishes information about HIV/AIDS in the *Morbidity and Mortality Weekly Report*. As an agency of the CDC, NPIN is a reference and referral service for information on HIV/AIDS and other sexually transmitted diseases. It collects, catalogs, processes, and electronically disseminates materials and information on the virus to organizations and people working in those fields in international, national, state, and local settings.

Concerned Women for America (CWA)

1015 15th Street NW, Suite 1100
Washington, DC 20005
(202) 488-7000 • fax: (202) 488-0806
website: www.cwfa.org

The CWA aims to promote biblical values throughout society in order to reverse what it believes is a decline in America's moral values. CWA supports abstinence-only sexual education and questions the efficacy of condoms in preventing AIDS. The organization publishes the magazine *Family Voice* as well as brochures, including "What Your Teacher Didn't Tell You About Abstinence."

Family Research Council (FRC)

801 G Street NW
Washington, DC 20001
(202) 393-2100 • fax: (202) 393-2134
website: www.frc.org

The FRC develops public policy that upholds the institutions of marriage and family; among the issues it supports is abstinence-only education. Publications on AIDS and abstinence-only education are available on the website, including "Abstinence Education Is the Key" and "Abstinence Works: Let's Give It a Chance."

Global AIDS Interfaith Alliance (GAIA)

PO Box 29110
San Francisco, CA 94129-0100
(415) 461-7196 • fax: (415) 461-9681
e-mail: info@thegaia.org
website: www.thegaia.org

GAIA is a nonprofit organization composed of AIDS researchers and doctors, religious leaders, and African medical officials, most of whom are associated with religion-based clinics and hospitals. The organization is concerned with infrastructure development and the training of prevention educators and personnel to conduct HIV testing and counseling. It also emphasizes the modification of values, structures, and practices that predispose women and girls to higher HIV infection rates than men, stigmatize ill people, and contribute to public denial. GAIA's website offers news and updates about AIDS.

Health, Education, AIDS Liaison (HEAL)

(416) 778-4207
e-mail: inquiries@healtoronto.com
website: www.healtoronto.com

HEAL is a network of international chapters that challenges the validity of the traditional HIV/AIDS hypothesis and efficacy of HIV drug treatments. HEAL believes that debate and open inquiry are fundamental parts of the scientific process and should not be abandoned to accommodate the current theory of HIV. Its website provides articles that question the link between HIV and AIDS and offers information about HIV tests, AIDS in Africa, and drug treatments.

Joint United Nations Programme on HIV/AIDS (UNAIDS)

20 Avenue Appia
Geneva 27 CH-1211
Switzerland
+41 22 791-3666 • fax: +41 22 791-4187
website: www.unaids.org

UNAIDS was created by the combination of six AIDS and health organizations. It is a leading advocate for the worldwide action against HIV/AIDS, and its global mission is to lead, strengthen, and support an expanded response to the AIDS epidemic that will prevent the spread of HIV, provide care and support for those infected and affected by HIV/AIDS, and alleviate the socioeconomic impact of the epidemic. UNAIDS produces many publications, including *AIDS at 30: Nations at the Crossroads*.

National AIDS Fund

1030 15th St. NW, Suite 860
Washington, DC 20005
(202) 408-4848 • fax: (202) 408-1818
e-mail: info@aidsfund.org
website: www.aidsfund.org

The National AIDS Fund seeks to eliminate HIV as a major health and social problem. Its members work in partnership with the public and private sectors to provide care and prevent new infections in communities and in the workplace by means of advocacy, grants, research, and education. The fund published the monthly newsletter *News from the National AIDS Fund*, which is also available through its website.

National Association of People with AIDS (NAPWA)

8401 Colesville Road, Suite 505
Silver Spring, MD 20910
(240) 247-0880 • fax: (240) 247-0574
website: www.napwa.org

NAPWA is an organization that represents people with HIV. Its members believe that it is the inalienable right of every person with HIV to have health care, be free of discrimination, have the right to a dignified death, be adequately housed, be protected from violence, and travel and immigrate regardless of country of origin or HIV status. The organization publishes *Strategic Plan*.

Bibliography of Books

Aids2013 Consortium — *AIDS: Taking a Long-Term View.* Upper Saddle River, NJ: FT Press, 2011.

Henry H. Bauer — *The Origin, Persistence, and Failings of HIV/AIDS Theory.* Jefferson, NC: McFarland, 2007.

Marvelyn Brown and Courtney Martin — *The Naked Truth: Young, Beautiful, and (HIV) Positive.* New York: HarperCollins, 2008.

Aine Collier — *The Humble Little Condom: A History.* Amherst, NY: Prometheus Books, 2007.

Rebecca Culshaw — *Science Sold Out: Does HIV Really Cause AIDS?* Berkeley, CA: North Atlantic Books, 2007.

Benjamin Dov Fleury-Steiner — *Dying Inside: The HIV/AIDS Ward at Limestone Prison.* Ann Arbor: University of Michigan Press, 2008.

Samuel Frimpong — *STD/HIV Prevention Action: Let's Protect Each Other.* Bloomington, IN: iUniverse, 2010.

Daniel Gebhardt — *I Am This One Walking Beside Me: Meditations of a Gay HIV Positive Man.* San Jose, CA: Resource, 2010.

Quinn Gentry — *Black Women's Risk for HIV: Rough Living.* New York: Routledge, 2007.

Susanna W. Grannis — *Hope Amidst Despair: HIV/AIDS-Affected Children in Sub-Saharan Africa.* London: Pluto, 2011.

Josefina Guardia — *Living Hell: The Truth About AIDS and HIV*. Bloomington, IN: iUniverse, 2011.

Victoria A. Harden — *AIDS at 30: A History*. Dulles, VA: Potomac Books, 2012.

Maureen E. Lyon and Laurence J. D'Angelo — *Teenagers, HIV, and AIDS: Insights from Youths Living with the Virus*. Westport, CT: Praeger, 2006.

Luc Montagnier — *Virus: The Co-discoverer of HIV Tracks Its Rampage and Charts the Future*. New York. Norton, 2008.

Peter Mugyenyi — *Genocide by Denial: How Profiteering from HIV/AIDS Killed Millions*. East Lansing: Michigan State University Press, 2008.

Elizabeth Pisani — *The Wisdom of Whores: Bureaucrats, Brothels, and the Business of AIDS*. New York: Norton, 2008.

Fran Quigley — *Walking Together, Walking Far: How a U.S. and African Medical School Partnership Is Winning the Fight Against HIV/AIDS*. Bloomington: Indiana University Press, 2009.

Vasu Reddy, Theo Sandfort, and Laetitia Rispel, eds. — *From Social Silence to Social Science: Same-Sex Sexuality, HIV & AIDS, and Gender in South Africa*. Cape Town, South Africa: Human Sciences Research Council, 2009.

Vaughn Ripley	*Survivor: One Man's Battle with HIV, Hemophilia, and Hepatitis C.* Bloomington, IN: iUniverse, 2010.
Paul E. Sax, Calvin J. Cohen, and Daniel R. Kuritzkes, eds.	*HIV Essentials.* Boston: Physicians' Press, 2010.
Shane Stanford	*A Positive Life: Living with HIV as a Pastor, Husband, and Father.* Grand Rapids, MI: Zondervan, 2010.
Matthew Waeit	*Intimacy and Responsibility: The Criminalisation of HIV Transmission.* New York: Routledge-Cavendish, 2007.

Index